FAMILY FOOD

This book is dedicated to all the bunnies ... the mums, dads, grandparents, aunties, uncles, big sisters/brothers, guardians, schoolteachers, childcare workers, hospital staff and healthcare practitioners who have the courage to step outside what is considered 'normal' in our society and reclaim their health and the health of those they care most about. There is a health revolution dawning and you are on the front lines of the battlefield.

FAMILY FOOD

130 DELICIOUS PALEO RECIPES FOR EVERY DAY

PETE EVANS

CONTENTS

INTRODUCTION

My family is one of the greatest joys of my life and nourishing them with delicious, nutritious food is a true pleasure and a responsibility that I don't take lightly. The eating habits that we teach our kids, starting from when they first begin exploring solids through to their teenage years, stay with them for life. It is so important that we help to set them on the right path and show them how to make healthy choices for themselves. This does not mean lecturing them on what they should or shouldn't be eating or forcing them to eat foods they don't want to. Food should be a celebration – something that brings people and families together. One of the best ways to encourage an interest in food and health is to get your kids involved in preparing meals and to make it fun. My daughters Chilli and Indii often help in the kitchen and always set the table, then we all sit down together and enjoy food and conversation. Making mealtimes a positive experience for the whole family is relatively easy to do and is a great first step in fostering healthy eating habits.

When it comes to what kind of food you should put on the table, I believe the best way to eat well and feel good is the 'paleo' way: applying paleolithic principles to the way we eat. This means packing our diet with foods our pre-agricultural ancestors ate and that humans have eaten over the longest span of our history – these are the foods our bodies are best adapted to. The paleo way also takes into account which foods provide the best fuel for our bodies, and encompasses the most recent advances in human longevity research.

In an (activated!) nutshell, a paleo diet is about minimising your consumption of sugary and starchy foods, moderating your protein intake, eating as much good-quality, unprocessed fat as you need to satisfy your appetite and support a healthy nervous system, and increasing your consumption of fibrous veggies. It's a beautifully simple style of eating that accentuates what I call 'real' food – unprocessed foods (foods that are in their natural state), such as raw, lightly cooked and/or fermented vegetables, high-quality meats, sustainable seafood, eggs, nuts and seeds. These are foods that our bodies are able to digest easily and they provide us with optimal nutrition at any age or stage in life. So, if you are thinking about going paleo, here are some tips to get you started.

7

- **Eat more veggies!** Eating paleo is all about eating foods that are rich with nutrients — and veggies are nutritional powerhouses so, with the exception of starchy vegetables like potatoes, you can pretty much eat as much of these as you want. Leafy green vegetables, such as kale, are particularly great, as they contain iron, calcium and lots of different vitamins, plus they also have antioxidant properties.

- **Cook your own food.** When you cook your own meals, you know exactly what you are eating and you know that there aren't any hidden surprises. I nearly always pack my own food for work, or when I travel on a plane, and I love to make breakfast, lunch and dinner whenever I can at home. Freezing soups and stocks for use later on and also eating leftovers for breakfast the next day is a great way to cook your own food when you don't have very much time.

- **Try replacing grains and legumes with healthier options.** Many people have trouble digesting cereal grains, such as wheat, rye and barley, while grain proteins, such as gluten, are a common source of allergies. A paleo-style diet avoids grains in order to improve the health of your gut bacteria, and emerging research shows that this can affect many aspects of your health. The paleo way also avoids legumes, as they are difficult for us to digest and contain high levels of lectins and phytic acid, which can interfere with our absorption of essential minerals and nutrients, so I avoid eating them. Cutting out grains and legumes from your diet might seem daunting but it isn't as hard as you think and I have heaps of suggestions to help you, such as replacing rice with cauliflower rice (page 180) or making muesli with nuts and seeds instead of cereal (page 14). And if you would like to read more about the effect of wheat and grains on our body, I recommend US doctor William Davis' compelling book *Wheat Belly*.

- **Know your oils.** When I cook, I prefer to use unrefined fats, such as coconut oil, ghee, duck fat or tallow. They are generally quite high in saturated fats, which used to be thought of as the enemy. Research now shows, however, that quality fats are good for us and that we should consume as much good-quality natural fat as is needed to satisfy our appetite and support the functioning of our brain and nervous system (for more information on quality fats, see page 286). I don't use vegetable, soybean, safflower, sunflower, corn, rice bran, cottonseed and canola oils as they are prone to rancidity, are highly processed and are high in omega-6 polyunsaturated fatty acids, which can be harmful when consumed in excess. Olive oil is great in salad dressing but should not be used for cooking as it has a low smoke point, which means heat degrades its beneficial compounds and creates potentially harmful ones.

- **Avoid refined sugars.** Sugar is added to so many processed foods these days that many people have no idea how much sugar they and their families consume on a daily basis. Eating too much sugar can increase your risk of weight gain, diabetes, cardiovascular disease and cancer. Excess sugar is also believed to age the body and cause wrinkles, and can contribute to digestive problems. For these reasons, I avoid refined sugar altogether, and only occasionally use small amounts of unrefined sweeteners, such as maple syrup and honey (see page 286). I feel much better for it, have more energy and never get the 3 pm slump I used to get when I ate sweet things.

INTRODUCTION

- **Enjoy fruit in small amounts.** Some people assume that transitioning to a paleo style of eating means cutting out fruit altogether, but this is not the case. Occasionally eating a small amount of seasonal fruit is optional (but not necessary) while following the paleo way. I usually opt for the occasional green apple and berries (berries are particularly great as they are high in antioxidants). Fresh juices are also fine occasionally – just make sure you go for a juice with lots of veggies and only a small amount of fruit in order to minimise the level of fructose.

- **Drink more water.** Our bodies are 75 per cent water so it makes sense that we need to drink lots of it! I always drink two glasses of filtered water when I first wake up. Dehydration is often mistaken for hunger, so next time you are hungry try having a glass or two of water first and see how you feel afterwards. And by replacing unhealthy beverages like soft drinks and coffee with filtered water you will already be on your way to better health.

- **Eat organic.** Organic produce is free from chemicals, pesticides and other contaminants. It is better for our bodies and the environment, and let's not forget the fact that it is just so darn delicious! Farmers markets are fabulous places to stock up on organic produce, direct from the farmer. Take the kids along and get them involved in choosing your veggies for the week – you might even discover new ingredients that you've never used before. I realise that organic produce isn't as readily available or as affordable as conventional produce, so if what you're after sometimes isn't available, don't be too hard on yourself if you have to choose the non-organic alternative.

- **Buy the best quality meat you can afford.** I use 100 per cent organic, humanely raised, pasture-fed-and-finished meats and organs, as they are sustainable and the healthiest option for both the planet and the human body. This meat will also be more tender and taste better. I love nose-to-tail eating (not just steaks but all of the other parts of the animal, which are cheap and so nutritious). I also source wild-caught seafood from unpolluted waters whenever possible, free-range poultry and pork (with no hormones or antibiotics) and wild game (if available). When shopping for organic meat ensure that it is certified; look for the labels 'Australian Certified Organic' or 'USDA Organic'.

- **Consult your GP or a trusted health professional.** It's important to consult your doctor or a health professional before making major changes to your diet. They will be familiar with both your current health and your medical history, so have a chat with them about the changes you'd like to make to double check they don't foresee any problems. Please note that consuming fermented vegetables as part of your daily diet can be problematic if you have certain medical conditions or are taking particular medications, so it's always best to consult your health professional before adding them to your diet.

The paleo way makes sense because it focuses on maximising the nutrients you are getting out of your food. For example, choosing a nut- and seed-based bread, packed with protein, fibre, omega-3 fatty acids and iron, rather than fluffy white bread that is high in carbohydrates and contains very little else that will nourish you. Because you can eat as much healthy fat as you need (in avocados, macadamias and coconut oil, for example), moderate amounts of high-quality protein, and as many fibre-filled veggies as you want, following the paleo way of eating doesn't leave you hungry. If fact, many people feel more satisfied than ever after transitioning to a paleo diet and this means that they are more likely to continue with it. On top of this, cutting out refined sugar will help to avoid both spikes in blood glucose levels and the fatigue you get from sugar crashes. To put it simply, transitioning to a paleo way of eating will leave you feeling amazing.

Aside from the fact that I love sharing healthy, flavoursome recipes, I felt inspired to write a family cookbook due to my passion for encouraging the nourishment of our little ones, as well as the frustration I feel about the so-called 'healthy' kids' cookbooks on the market. Many of these books recommend using large amounts of processed ingredients such as sugar and white flour, which I believe are not the best choices if we want to provide our kids with energy and nutrition for their growing bodies and minds. I felt compelled to create a family cookbook that empowers parents and children with an understanding of food and nutrition; a book that enlightens and inspires a return to balance, sustainability and vibrant health.

Kids are never too young to start learning about food and nutrition, so I encourage you to begin that conversation with them as soon as possible. My beautiful daughters, Chilli and Indii, love eating healthy food, but still sometimes ask why I don't let them have any of the 'bad stuff' – store-bought lollies, chocolates and chips. When they first asked this question, I told them a story to help them understand.

'Let's imagine you both had a little bunny rabbit and you knew that if you fed your bunny plenty of grass and vegetables and gave it clean water, that it would live a long and healthy life, because they are the best kinds of foods to keep your bunny nourished, happy and truly fit as a fiddle. What would you do if I then gave you the choice to feed your bunny some lollies (which it was very eager to eat), even though you knew that there was a good chance that the lollies could make the bunny less likely to live a long, healthy and happy life?'

Kids are very smart, and both of the girls immediately replied 'Grass and vegetables of course, Daddy!'. And they said that they would never, ever feed the bunny lollies. I told the girls that I was proud of the choice they had made, and then I went on to tell them that *they* are actually my precious little bunnies, and it is exactly the same situation. The best part of this story is that Chilli and Indii both fully comprehend the fact that they need to treat their bodies with respect and kindness. Of course, they will be offered lollies and other unhealthy foods from time to time, but we are trying to gently teach them to take responsibility for their own lives, to make educated choices and to not always follow what everyone else is doing. And I'm happy to say – so far, so good!

I know that changing the way you cook and eat can be a bit daunting, so in the beginning it makes sense to stick to familiar dishes – with a paleo twist of course! For this reason, I've included plenty of traditional family favourites in the following pages – such as roasts, fresh salads, 'pasta' (without the wheat – see page 154), meatballs and even party pies (page 76) – all without the unnecessary ingredients. There's also a chapter on kids' lunches with heaps of ideas to jazz up their lunchboxes. Just make sure that you check the food allergy policy at your child's school. Many schools these days are nut-free zones, so if the recipe does include nuts, I recommend either substituting seeds or simply saving these recipes for the weekend.

Transitioning to a paleo way of eating doesn't mean that you and your kids have to go without treats, either – there are plenty of options other than lollies and chocolates, and I've included a number of recipes for tasty but healthy treats to have occasionally (see the Snacks and Sweets chapters). And although some of the paleo ingredients might be unfamiliar at first, once you try them and start using them in your everyday cooking, you'll be won over and feel great.

INTRODUCTION

I wholeheartedly believe that part of our responsibility as parents is motivating our kids to assist in the kitchen and for this reason all the recipes in this book are designed to be prepared alongside your kids – whether it's picking the leaves off herbs, combining ingredients or rolling a mixture into balls, there's always a job that's perfect for little ones to enjoy, so that they can feel a sense of achievement and an all-important connection to their food too. I'm really proud of the recipes in this book and I hope you are able to take inspiration from the dishes that follow. I've tried to make them straightforward, accessible, affordable and – most importantly – downright YUMMY! So, let's jump into the kitchen to get this health revolution started – and hopefully create some magical food memories with your family along the way.

Cheers,
Pete Evans

www.thepaleoway.com
Keep cooking for life with love and laughter!

My partner, Nic, and I love spending time together in the kitchen, cooking delicious and healthy meals for our family and friends.

BREAKFAST

Anyone who has my book *Healthy Every Day* will be familiar with this recipe, as a similar one appears in it. This time, however, I've added dried apricots and cranberries to make it even more delicious. This is my daughter Chilli's favourite muesli and I encourage you to make this with your kids. Get them involved in the entire process all the way to making the nut milk.

ALMOND AND GOJI BERRY MUESLI

100 g (⅔ cup) almonds

80 g (½ cup) macadamia nuts

50 g (¼ cup) buckwheat*

3 tablespoons sunflower seeds

3 tablespoons pumpkin seeds

1 tablespoon sesame seeds

2 tablespoons goji berries

4 dried apricots, diced

2 tablespoons dried cranberries

2 tablespoons flaxseeds*

2 tablespoons coconut oil, melted

1 teaspoon ground cinnamon

½ teaspoon ground ginger

pinch of sea salt

2 tablespoons honey, or to taste

chopped banana, to serve

nut milk (to make your own, see page 258) or coconut milk, to serve

sliced strawberries, to serve

* *See Glossary*

Place the nuts, buckwheat and sunflower, pumpkin and sesame seeds in a large bowl. Cover with filtered water at room temperature and soak for 7 hours. Also place the goji berries, dried apricots and cranberries in a small bowl and soak in filtered water overnight.

Preheat the oven to the lowest temperature possible (40–50°C) and line a large baking tray with baking paper.

Drain the nuts, buckwheat, seeds and soaked dried fruit and rinse well. Place on a clean tea towel or paper towel and pat dry. Transfer to a food processor and pulse 3–5 times to your desired consistency (I don't process it for too long as I like to keep it a bit chunky). Add the flaxseeds, coconut oil, cinnamon, ginger, salt and honey and pulse to combine.

Spread the nut mixture out thinly on the prepared tray and place in the oven for 6–8 hours, or until your desired level of crunch is reached. Carefully give your muesli a light toss every couple of hours and make sure it is well spread out when baking.

Remove the muesli from the oven and allow to cool on the tray before breaking into small pieces. Transfer to an airtight glass container and store for up to 4 weeks.

To serve, mix through some chopped banana and add some milk and strawberries or other seasonal fruit of your choice.

SERVES 4

I am not one for eating dairy; in fact, less than 40 per cent of the people on this planet have the ability to digest dairy proteins. For about 3 million years we thrived without consuming the milk of other animals. This leads me to believe that we do not need dairy in any way, shape or form to be healthy. Recent research has shown that rates of osteoporosis are actually higher in populations that consume dairy products compared to those that don't. This dairy-free yoghurt is a great substitute for regular yoghurt and, served with a simple fruit salad, makes a delicious and satisfying breakfast.

FRUIT SALAD WITH COCONUT YOGHURT

2 kiwi fruit, peeled and cut into
1 cm pieces

1 mango, peeled and cut into
1 cm pieces

1 custard apple, peeled and cut
into 1 cm pieces

½ pineapple, peeled and cut into
1 cm pieces

400 g seedless watermelon,
cut into 1 cm pieces

80 g (½ cup) blueberries

2 tablespoons chopped mint leaves

black chia seeds*, to serve

COCONUT YOGHURT

flesh and water of 4 young
green coconuts*

juice of 2 lemons or limes

1–2 vanilla pods, split and seeds
scraped

yacon syrup*, maple syrup or
honey, to taste

2 probiotic capsules*

* See Glossary

To make the coconut yoghurt, combine the coconut flesh, one-third of the coconut water, the lemon or lime juice, vanilla seeds and sweetener to taste. Blend until smooth and creamy. Depending on the consistency you prefer, you can add more coconut water.

Open your probiotic capsules, pour into the blender and give one final quick whiz. Pour into a 1-litre glass jar, cover with paper towel and allow to sit for 6–12 hours at room temperature so that the bacteria can proliferate (break down the yoghurt). The longer you leave it, the tangier the yoghurt becomes. (This recipe makes about 600 ml – any leftover yoghurt can be stored in the fridge for up to 2 weeks.)

To make the fruit salad, layer the kiwi fruit, mango, custard apple, pineapple, watermelon, blueberries and mint in four glasses or bowls. Top with a generous amount of the coconut yoghurt and sprinkle over some chia seeds to finish.

SERVES 4

This chia porridge is considered a bit of a treat in our house and I like to play around with different flavours each time I make it. Cinnamon is a favourite, but I also use turmeric, sumac, ginger, cloves, chilli, star anise, cardamom and saffron. Then add nuts (macadamias, walnuts, almonds, Brazil nuts, hazelnuts or pecans) and fruit (berries, coconut, cacao, carob, tamarind, citrus fruits, tropical fruits or dried fruits).

CHIA PORRIDGE

100 g (¾ cup) black or white chia seeds*

500 ml (2 cups) coconut milk or almond milk, plus extra to serve

1 tablespoon honey or coconut sugar, plus extra to serve

1 vanilla pod, split and seeds scraped

½ teaspoon ground cinnamon, plus extra to dust

mixed berries (raspberries, blackberries, strawberries and blueberries), to serve

coconut flakes, to serve

* See Glossary

Place the chia seeds in a saucepan with the milk, honey or sugar and vanilla seeds, mix well and bring to a simmer over medium heat. Reduce the heat to low, cover and simmer for 5 minutes until the porridge is light and fluffy. Stir occasionally to prevent the porridge from sticking to the bottom of the pan.

Fluff the porridge with a fork and allow to cool a little before stirring in the cinnamon.

Spoon into two bowls and scatter over the berries and coconut. Add a drizzle of honey or a sprinkle of sugar if you like, dust a little more cinnamon on top and finish with some extra milk.

SERVES 2

These pancakes are a real treat in our household. Mixed berries go beautifully with any type of nut – in this recipe I've used hazelnuts, but you could substitute any ground nuts. I like to top these with some fresh coconut yoghurt (page 16) or homemade paleo ice cream (page 241) to create that amazing contrast between something warm and something cold. We probably only eat these once every month or so, as they are pretty heavy in the fructose department and not really an everyday kind of breakfast.

MIXED BERRY AND HAZELNUT PANCAKES

2 eggs

3 tablespoons coconut milk

¼ teaspoon vanilla powder

1 tablespoon honey

55 g (½ cup) hazelnut meal

1 teaspoon baking powder

3 teaspoons coconut flour

120 g (½ cup) mixed berries, roughly chopped

pinch of sea salt

1 tablespoon coconut oil or ghee*, plus extra to serve

TO SERVE

maple syrup or honey

lemon juice

Coconut Yoghurt (page 16)

mixed berries (such as raspberries, blueberries, mulberries and strawberries)

coconut flakes, toasted (optional)

* See Glossary

In a small bowl, whisk the eggs for about 2 minutes, or until frothy. Mix in the coconut milk, vanilla and honey. Set aside.

In a large bowl, combine the hazelnut meal, baking powder, coconut flour, berries and salt.

Stir the wet mixture into the dry ingredients until the coconut flour is incorporated and the berries are evenly mixed through.

Grease a large frying pan with a little ghee or coconut oil and pour ¼ cup of batter for each pancake into the pan (you'll probably only be able to cook two pancakes at a time). Cook over medium heat for 2 minutes, or until the tops dry out slightly and the bottoms start to brown. Flip and cook for another minute, then transfer the pancakes to a plate, cover and keep warm. Repeat until all the batter is used.

Serve the hot pancakes with maple syrup or honey, lemon juice, coconut yoghurt, berries and coconut flakes (if using).

SERVES 2

Bread is one of the hardest foods for people to give up as it has usually been a part of their diet for as long as they can remember – toast with lashings of butter and jam for breakfast, sandwiches at lunchtime and bread (or if you were lucky, garlic bread!) as a side for dinner. Embracing the paleo way of life is not about going without, but about removing nutritionally poor foods, such as carb-laden bread, from our diet and embracing healthier options. Here is a great substitute for our daily bread that not only tastes a million times better, but will be a nourishing addition to your diet. It is full of protein and fibre from the nuts and seeds, as well as omega-3 fatty acids and calcium from the chia seeds and LSA.

SEED AND NUT BREAD

3 tablespoons sunflower seeds (activated if possible, see page 200), chopped, plus 1 tablespoon extra, for sprinkling

3 tablespoons pumpkin seeds (activated if possible, see page 200), chopped, plus 1 tablespoon extra, for sprinkling

1 tablespoon black or white chia seeds*, plus 1 tablespoon extra, for sprinkling

50 g (⅓ cup) almonds (activated if possible, see page 200), chopped

150 g (1½ cups) almond meal

3 tablespoons LSA*

1 teaspoon bicarbonate of soda

2 tablespoons coconut flour

6 eggs

1 tablespoon honey (optional)

1 tablespoon apple cider vinegar

4 tablespoons coconut oil

1 teaspoon sea salt

* See Glossary

Preheat the oven to 160°C. Grease a 20 cm × 10 cm loaf tin and line the base and sides with baking paper.

Mix the sunflower, pumpkin and chia seeds in a large bowl. Stir through the almonds, almond meal, LSA, bicarbonate of soda and coconut flour. Add the eggs, honey (if using), vinegar, coconut oil and salt and mix well to combine. The mixture will resemble a batter rather than a dough.

Pour the dough into the prepared loaf tin and smooth out evenly with a spatula. Sprinkle the extra seeds on top. Bake for 45–50 minutes, or until golden and a skewer inserted in the centre comes out clean. (You will need to do the skewer test because this bread is much denser than regular bread and won't sound hollow when you tap it.) Remove from the oven and allow to cool in the tin before turning out.

You can store this bread in the fridge for up to 5 days, or in the freezer for up to 3 months.

SERVES 8

My daughters absolutely love boiled eggs. And I cannot think of a better way to start their day than with a protein-and-good-fat-packed parcel of goodness. Chop up some herbs, such as chives, dill or parsley, and sprinkle them over the runny yolk. This egg bread is a great recipe for those people who would like to try a paleo diet but are worried about how they are going to survive without bread! I fully understand the resistance to giving up our daily bread, and with this recipe – kindly shared by my good friends Marlies and Jai from Paleo Café – you won't feel like you are missing out on anything. Try wrapping some jamon or prosciutto around the toast before dipping into the egg.

SOFT-BOILED EGGS WITH EGG BREAD SOLDIERS

4 eggs

coconut oil or ghee*, at room temperature, to serve

EGG BREAD (MAKES 1 LOAF)

185 ml (¾ cup) coconut oil or ghee*, melted

15 eggs

55 g (½ cup) flaxseed meal*

60 g (½ cup) coconut flour

¾ teaspoon baking powder

¾ teaspoon garlic powder

¾ teaspoon sea salt flakes

¾ teaspoon cracked black pepper

* See Glossary

To make the egg bread, preheat the oven to 180°C. Line a 22 cm × 12 cm loaf tin with baking paper.

Place the coconut oil or ghee and 10 of the eggs in a large bowl and beat with an electric mixer on high speed for 2–3 minutes, or until slightly aerated. Reduce the speed to low and add the flaxseed meal, coconut flour, baking powder, garlic powder, salt and pepper. Continue beating for a further 2 minutes. The mixture will look a bit curdled at this stage, but that's fine.

Return the speed to high and add the remaining five eggs one at a time, beating well after each addition, until the mixture is fluffy.

Pour the mixture into the loaf tin and bake for 25–30 minutes, or until it is lightly browned and a skewer inserted into the centre of the bread comes out clean. Turn the loaf out onto a wire rack to cool.

Place the four eggs in a saucepan of cold water, cover and bring to the boil over high heat. Reduce the heat and simmer for 4 minutes to get lovely, soft yolks.

Transfer the eggs to egg cups. Using a spoon, carefully remove the tops from the eggs.

Meanwhile, cut four thick slices of egg bread and toast until golden. Spread the toast with some coconut oil or ghee and cut into finger-sized portions. Serve immediately with the eggs. The remaining egg bread will keep in an airtight container in the fridge for up to 1 week or in the freezer for up to 3 months.

SERVES 4

Too many sweet potatoes are a no-no if you are trying to lose weight; however, if you are active and your kids are surfing or skateboarding before and after school, running the dog, riding bikes, swimming and basically living life as a kid should, then a few sweet potato fritters will nicely satisfy everyone's hunger. I like to have these for breakfast and team them with eggs and a big pile of sautéed greens, such as kale, asparagus or zucchini. You can add other veggies to the fritter mix. Try onion, zucchini, carrot, Jerusalem artichoke, beetroot and pumpkin and perhaps some tuna or roast chicken to make them more versatile. Add a soft-boiled egg and some raw veggies and these turn into a wonderful lunchbox option for the kids.

SWEET POTATO ROSTI

4 eggs

2–4 tablespoons coconut oil or other good-quality fat*

1 tablespoon chopped flat-leaf parsley leaves

SWEET POTATO ROSTI

600 g sweet potato, peeled and grated

2 eggs, at room temperature

sea salt and freshly ground black pepper

See Glossary

Fill a small saucepan with water and bring to the boil over high heat. Reduce the heat to low so that the water is simmering, then add the eggs and cook for 5 minutes. Drain and, when cool enough to handle, peel the eggs under cold running water. Set aside.

To make the sweet potato rosti, squeeze all the excess moisture from the grated sweet potato using a sieve and place in a bowl. Add the eggs and salt and pepper and mix well.

Heat 1 tablespoon of oil or fat in a non-stick frying pan over medium–high. Spoon in about 2 tablespoons of the rosti mixture and shape into a patty. Cook for 2 minutes, pressing with a spatula to flatten slightly, or until golden on the underside. Turn and cook the other side for another 2 minutes until crisp and golden. Repeat to make another three rosti.

Cut each peeled egg in half and serve with a rosti and a sprinkle of parsley.

SERVES 4

I adore the simple things in life. And what could be simpler than a delicious bacon, lettuce and tomato sandwich? First thing you need is some good-quality paleo bread (no grains or sugar) – see pages 23 and 24. Then it comes down to how crispy you like your bacon, how thickly sliced you like your tomatoes and what type of lettuce you wish to use (iceberg, cos, butter, coral and mâche are great, or you may like something with a bit more bite like rocket, radicchio, witlof, dandelion leaves or watercress). Optional extras are whatever your imagination can conjure up, but a few items to consider are sliced avocado or guacamole, homemade mayo or aioli, fermented vegetables and, of course, fresh herbs like basil, chives, tarragon, chervil or dill.

PALEO BLT

8 slices of Egg Bread (page 24)

1 tablespoon coconut oil or other good-quality fat*

4 rashers of bacon

4 tablespoons aioli (to make your own, see page 172)

8 baby cos lettuce leaves

2 vine-ripened tomatoes, sliced

2 tablespoons tomato relish (to make your own, see recipe below)

sea salt and freshly ground black pepper

TOMATO RELISH

1 tablespoon macadamia oil

1 onion, chopped

1 tablespoon yellow mustard seeds

3 garlic cloves, chopped

1 long red chilli, chopped

1 tablespoon grated ginger

1 tablespoon ground turmeric

6 vine-ripened tomatoes, diced

2½ tablespoons red wine vinegar

1½ tablespoons honey (optional)

* See Glossary

Toast the bread slices in a toaster until light golden brown. Alternatively, toast in the oven at 200°C for 5–8 minutes (check after 4 minutes), or until pale golden.

Meanwhile, heat the oil or fat in a frying pan over medium–high heat, add the bacon and fry for 2 minutes on each side until golden and crispy.

Spread about a tablespoon of aioli on one side of the toasted egg bread slices, then top four slices with the lettuce, tomato, bacon and tomato relish. Season with salt and pepper and place the remaining toast slices, aioli side down, on top. Cut the sandwiches in half and devour.

TOMATO RELISH

To make your own tomato relish, heat the oil in a saucepan over medium heat, add the onion and cook for a few minutes, or until lightly browned. Add the mustard seeds, garlic, chilli, ginger and turmeric and cook for 1 minute, or until fragrant and the mustard seeds start to pop. Add the tomato and cook for 5 minutes, or until softened. Add the red wine vinegar and honey (if using) and cook, stirring regularly, for about 10–15 minutes, or until the liquid has reduced by half. Season with salt and pepper and cool. Leftover tomato relish can be stored in an airtight container in the fridge for up to 2 months.

SERVES 4

The first time I tried nasi goreng – a delicious mixture of seafood and meat with egg, spices and vegetables – I was blown away. I couldn't believe that this was a breakfast dish in countries such as Indonesia and Malaysia. I am so excited to share my paleo nasi goreng recipe. I've changed it from a GI-spiking rice dish to one that will sustain you for a lot longer. And I believe that it is even better than the original. If you are avoiding all types of soy, even tamari and miso, then simply replace it with coconut aminos or increase the quantity of sugar-free fish sauce to your taste.

NASI GORENG

600 g cauliflower, roughly chopped

4 tablespoons coconut oil

350 g chicken thigh fillets, skin left on, cut into 2 cm pieces

150 g bacon, cut into 2 cm pieces

4 spring onions, thinly sliced

1 long red chilli, deseeded and finely chopped

2 garlic cloves, crushed

1 small carrot, finely diced

1 celery stalk, finely diced

1 teaspoon shrimp paste*

80 g Chinese cabbage (wong bok), finely shredded

150 g shelled and deveined cooked baby prawns

80 g bean sprouts

4 tablespoons fried shallots or garlic (to make your own, see below)

3 tablespoons tamari or coconut aminos*

1 teaspoon honey (optional)

1 tablespoon fish sauce

1 teaspoon tamarind* paste

4 eggs

salt and freshly ground black pepper

lime wedges, to serve

FRIED SHALLOTS OR GARLIC

250 ml (1 cup) coconut oil

4 French shallots or garlic cloves, thinly sliced

* See Glossary

Place the cauliflower in a food processor and pulse into small granules – it should resemble rice. Set aside.

Place a large wok or deep frying pan over medium–high heat, add 1 tablespoon of the coconut oil and heat until just smoking. Add half the chicken and stir-fry for 3 minutes, or until brown and just cooked. Transfer to a bowl, then stir-fry the remaining chicken in another tablespoon of oil. Transfer to the bowl. Add the bacon to the pan and stir-fry for 3 minutes until golden and crispy. Transfer to the bowl with the cooked chicken. Add another tablespoon of oil to the pan and heat over medium heat. Add the spring onion, chilli and garlic and stir-fry for 30 seconds. Add the carrot and celery and stir-fry for a further 3 minutes.

Return the chicken and bacon to the pan, then add the shrimp paste, cabbage and prawns and stir-fry for 2 minutes, or until the cabbage wilts. Add the cauliflower rice, bean sprouts, 2 tablespoons of fried shallots, the tamari or coconut aminos, honey (if using), fish sauce and tamarind. Stir-fry for 2 minutes until heated through. Transfer to a bowl and keep warm.

Heat half of the remaining oil or fat in a large non-stick frying pan over medium–high heat. Crack two eggs into the pan and fry until the whites set and the yolks begin to harden. Transfer the eggs to a plate and repeat with the remaining eggs and oil. Season with salt and pepper.

Spoon the nasi goreng into four serving bowls, top each one with a fried egg and the remaining fried shallots. Serve with lime wedges.

FRIED SHALLOTS OR GARLIC

To make your own fried shallots or garlic, melt the oil in a small saucepan over medium heat. Add the shallots or garlic and cook for 2–3 minutes until golden. Remove with a slotted spoon and drain on paper towel. (You can re-use the oil for sautéing vegetables or cooking meat, chicken or fish.)

SERVES 4

I love eating a hearty, warming meal in the cooler months and this versatile dish can be made in individual portions or in a big roasting tray that will feed an army. You can have everything done the day before and plated up in a baking dish and then just crack the eggs into it and pop it in the oven when you wake up. Experiment with different spices and proteins – try using lamb, pork, beef, chicken, prawns, clams and squid – or keep it vegetarian and use leftover roast veggies.

MOROCCAN BAKED EGGS WITH CHERMOULA

2 tablespoons coconut oil

1 red onion, finely chopped

1 red capsicum, finely chopped

2 garlic cloves, crushed

2 teaspoons ground cumin

2 teaspoons ground coriander

1 teaspoon ground cinnamon

2 teaspoons smoked paprika

600 g lamb mince

juice of 1 lemon

250 g (1 cup) diced tomatoes

salt and freshly ground black pepper

1 handful of baby spinach

4 eggs

coriander leaves, to serve

dried chilli flakes, to serve (optional)

CHERMOULA

1 large handful of coriander leaves, chopped

1 large handful of flat-leaf parsley leaves, chopped

1 large handful of mint leaves, chopped

3 garlic cloves, chopped

2 teaspoons ground cumin

2 teaspoons ground coriander

1 teaspoon paprika

1 small red chilli, chopped

3 tablespoons lemon juice

125 ml (½ cup) olive oil

salt and freshly ground black pepper

In a tagine or large saucepan, heat the coconut oil over medium heat. Add the onion, capsicum and garlic and sauté for 3–4 minutes, or until softened. Stir in the spices and cook for 1 minute until fragrant. Add the mince and cook, stirring to break up any lumps, for at least 3–4 minutes until brown. Stir in the lemon juice and tomatoes, season with salt and pepper, then turn down the heat to a simmer and cook for 5 minutes. Remove from the heat, then fold through the spinach.

Create four holes in the mince using a wooden spoon and crack an egg into each. (If you are making individual serves, spoon the mince into four ramekins, make a hole in each one and crack an egg into each.) Season the eggs with salt and pepper, cover the pan with a lid and cook for 5–7 minutes, or until the eggs are cooked to your liking.

Meanwhile, make the chermoula. Mix the herbs, garlic, spices, chilli and lemon juice in a food processor. While the motor is running, drizzle in the oil and process until smooth. Season with salt and pepper.

To finish, drizzle some chermoula over the eggs and scatter on the coriander and chilli flakes (if using). Leftover chermoula can be stored in an airtight container in the fridge for 3–4 days.

SERVES 4

When you're following a paleo way of eating, not every meal needs to be grass-fed rib eye from cattle raised on Tasmania's green pastures (save that for birthdays and celebrations). In fact, most meals use cheaper (secondary) cuts of meat and organ meats (offal). This humble frittata is a really inexpensive but delicious dish that is great for breakfast, lunch, dinner or a snack. If you don't have any leftover roast meat, use ham or bacon instead. In fact, you can add anything you like. Try zucchini, basil and toasted nuts, or last night's leftover roast chicken with some asparagus, roast pumpkin and thyme, or add some smoked trout with spinach and horseradish, or . . . you get the picture!

BUBBLE AND SQUEAK FRITTATA

10 eggs

125 ml (½ cup) coconut cream

sea salt and freshly ground black pepper

3 tablespoons coconut oil or other good-quality fat*

1 large onion, sliced

2 garlic cloves, crushed

200 g leftover roast lamb (or other leftover roast meat, such as chicken, beef or pork)

200 g cooked veggies (pumpkin, sweet potato, carrot or other leftover vegetables), cut into cubes

300 g cabbage, kale, brussels sprouts or other leftover greens, shredded

2 tablespoons chopped flat-leaf parsley leaves

* See Glossary

Preheat the oven to 180°C. Line a deep baking tray with baking paper, allowing the paper to extend a few centimetres above the sides.

Crack the eggs into a bowl, whisk lightly with the coconut cream and season well with salt and pepper. Set aside.

Heat the coconut oil or other fat in a large frying pan over medium heat. Add the onion and garlic and cook for 3–5 minutes until soft and slightly golden. Stir in the leftover meat, vegetables and parsley and cook gently for 2–3 minutes until heated through. Season with some salt and pepper, transfer to the prepared tray, then pour in the egg mixture. Place in the oven and bake for 30 minutes, or until golden on top and the egg is cooked.

Leave the frittata to cool for at least 10 minutes, then either cut into portions in the tray or use the baking paper to lift it out in one piece onto a chopping board or platter. Cut into portions and serve.

SERVES 6

Why on earth do I have a recipe for bacon and eggs in this cookbook? Well, the simple answer is that my family eats this once a week at home. Do I have a secret to cooking bacon and eggs that is different from the way you do? Well, probably not! So, again, why is this recipe here? The simple answer is that cooking does not have to be difficult or fancy. It should be accessible and achievable, no matter how much of a wizard you are in the kitchen, and I want to share exactly what I cook at home with you.

BACON AND EGGS WITH SLOW-ROASTED CHERRY TOMATOES

6 cherry tomatoes, halved

½ teaspoon dried oregano

1 garlic clove, crushed

4 tablespoons coconut oil or other good-quality fat*, melted

sea salt and freshly ground black pepper

4 rashers of bacon

4 eggs

½ ripe avocado, cut into 2 cm cubes

1 teaspoon lemon juice

1 tablespoon olive oil

flat-leaf parsley leaves, to serve

* See Glossary

Preheat the oven to 120°C. Line a baking tray with baking paper.

Arrange the cherry tomatoes, cut-side up, on the prepared tray. Sprinkle on the oregano and garlic and drizzle 1 tablespoon of the coconut oil or fat over the top. Season with salt and pepper. Bake in the oven for 30–35 minutes, or until the tomatoes have shrivelled slightly but are still juicy.

Heat 1 tablespoon of the coconut oil or fat in a non-stick frying pan over medium heat, add the bacon and cook for 2–3 minutes on each side until golden. If you like your bacon very crispy, cook for longer. Remove from the pan and keep warm.

Wipe the pan clean and reheat over medium heat with the remaining coconut oil or fat. Crack in the eggs and fry for 2 minutes until the eggwhite is set, or the eggs are cooked to your liking.

Place the avocado in a small bowl and pour in the lemon juice and olive oil. Gently toss and set aside.

Arrange the bacon and eggs on serving plates, then top with the avocado, oven-roasted cherry tomatoes and season with salt and pepper. Garnish with the parsley and serve.

SERVES 2

Breakfast burritos have become pretty popular over the last decade. I wanted to include a version that wasn't full of cheese and wheat. In my mind, a burrito is all about the filling: sensational meat, flavoured with delicious aromatic spices that send your tastebuds on a culinary journey. Then it is up to you how you want to finish it. I've teamed it here with a Mexican aioli and avocado salsa, but you could try a tomato salsa, some coleslaw or fermented chilli sauce. Yum! And I know I have said this is a breakfast burrito, but you should feel free to eat this any time of the day or night.

BREAKFAST BURRITO WITH CHIPOTLE AIOLI

1 tablespoon coconut oil or other good-quality fat*

300 g beef mince

1 teaspoon ground cumin

¼ teaspoon ground coriander

½ teaspoon chipotle chilli powder*

½ teaspoon onion powder

½ yellow capsicum, diced

1 tomato, diced

4 Coconut Flour Tortillas (page 141)

2 handfuls of wild rocket

4 boiled eggs, peeled and quartered

CHIPOTLE AIOLI

250 g (1 cup) aioli (to make your own, see page 172)

2 chipotle chillies* in adobo sauce

1 tablespoon adobo sauce*

AVOCADO SALSA

1 avocado, diced

1 tomato, diced

1 tablespoon finely chopped red onion

2 tablespoons chopped coriander leaves

juice of 1 lime

1 tablespoon extra-virgin olive oil

sea salt and freshly ground black pepper

* See Glossary

Melt 1 tablespoon of oil or fat in a frying pan over medium–high heat. Add the beef, spices, onion powder, capsicum and tomato and cook, stirring occasionally to break up any lumps, for 6–8 minutes until the mince is cooked through and the tomato has broken down.

To make the chipotle aioli, use a hand-held blender to blend all the ingredients until smooth. (Add more aioli if the flavour is too spicy for your liking, or add more chipotles if you prefer the aioli to be extra spicy.)

To make the avocado salsa, combine the avocado, tomato, onion, coriander, lime juice and olive oil in a bowl and mix gently. Season with salt and pepper and set aside.

Fill the tortillas with a good amount of the beef, spoon on some avocado salsa, then add a drizzle of chipotle aioli and top with some rocket leaves and egg. Wrap up the tortillas and serve.

SERVES 4

Paleo eating does not have to be expensive. Sure, the meat from humanely and sustainably raised animals will cost more than that from feedlot farms, but when you think about the real cost of this kind of farming, it is worth paying a bit extra for ethically raised meat. When you buy your mince, make sure there is a good amount of fat in it, as low-fat mince will make your sausages dry and tasteless.

LICORICE SAUSAGES WITH HOMEMADE BARBECUE SAUCE

1 teaspoon sea salt

½ teaspoon whole cloves

¼ teaspoon coriander seeds

¼ teaspoon white peppercorns

1 tablespoon licorice root powder*

4 thyme sprigs, leaves picked and finely chopped

1 tablespoon chopped flat-leaf parsley leaves

2 garlic cloves, crushed

500 g pork mince

1 tablespoon coconut oil

barbecue sauce (to make your own, see recipe below), to serve

tomato wedges, to serve

rocket leaves, to serve

BARBECUE SAUCE

100 g tomato paste

3 tablespoons apple cider vinegar

2 tablespoons Dijon mustard or Fermented Mustard (page 177)

4½ tablespoons honey (optional)

½ teaspoon smoked paprika

160 ml (⅔ cup) tamari

2 garlic cloves, crushed

pinch of ground cloves

pinch of ground cinnamon

sea salt and freshly ground black pepper

* See Glossary

Using a spice grinder or a mortar and pestle, grind the salt, cloves, coriander seeds and peppercorns into a fine powder.

Place the spice mixture in a bowl and stir in the licorice root powder, thyme, parsley and garlic, along with 2 tablespoons of water. Add the pork and mix by hand to combine. Set aside for 15 minutes to allow the flavours to infuse.

Shape the pork mixture into finger-sized logs.

Heat the coconut oil in a large frying pan over medium–high heat. Add the sausages in batches and cook for about 3 minutes on each side, or until cooked through and golden brown.

Serve the sausages with the barbecue sauce and rocket and tomato.

BARBECUE SAUCE

To make your own barbecue sauce, place the tomato paste, vinegar, mustard, honey (if using), paprika, tamari, garlic and spices in a saucepan over medium heat and bring to the boil. Turn the heat to low and simmer, stirring occasionally, for 15 minutes, or until the mixture thickens. Season with salt and pepper and leave to cool. Leftover barbecue sauce can be stored in an airtight container in the fridge for up to 2 weeks.

SERVES 4

BABY & TODDLER FOOD

Avocado and banana

Tropical fruit

Apple, peach and berry

These have been frozen in an ice cube tray for later use.

Chicken, apricot and sweet potato

Roasted pumpkin

Liver and sweet potato

BABY & TODDLER FOOD

Introducing your baby to solids can be a somewhat daunting endeavour, so please consult your child health professional for advice on which foods you should be introducing when. Feel free to double or triple the quantities of these purees and mashes and freeze them for later use in ice cube trays. Some of these recipes feature fruit, but please go easy as children don't need a huge amount of it. It's crucial to use homemade stock as store-bought stocks are loaded with salt and preservatives. If you don't have any homemade stock, use water instead.

Tropical fruit

¼ rockmelon, chopped
¼ papaya, chopped
¼ mango, chopped

Blend the fruit in a food processor until smooth. Store in an airtight container in the fridge for 3–4 days.

MAKES 8 PORTIONS

Liver and sweet potato

240 g chicken livers, trimmed
1 small sweet potato, diced
250 ml (1 cup) homemade chicken stock (page 86) or water

Place the livers and sweet potato in a small saucepan and pour in the stock or water. Bring to the boil, then lower the heat and simmer for 5–8 minutes, or until the sweet potato is tender and the liver is cooked through. Use a hand-held blender to puree until smooth. Store in an airtight container in the fridge for up to 2 days.

MAKES 6 PORTIONS

Chicken, apricot and sweet potato

2 chicken thigh fillets, diced
4 fresh apricots or 4 dried apricots (optional)
2 tablespoons coconut oil or other good-quality fat*
500 ml (2 cups) homemade chicken stock (page 86) or water
350 g sweet potato, chopped

If using fresh apricots, remove the stones and chop. Heat the oil in a saucepan over medium heat, add the chicken and sear for 1 minute on each side until brown. Add the stock or water, sweet potato and apricots (if using). Bring to the boil, reduce the heat to low and simmer for 15–20 minutes, or until the sweet potato is tender. Use a hand-held blender to puree until smooth. Store in an airtight container in the fridge for up to 2 days.

MAKES 6–8 PORTIONS

Avocado and banana

1 ripe avocado
2 small bananas (optional)
80–160 ml breast milk (optional)

Mash the avocado with the banana and milk (if using) until nice and smooth. Store in an airtight container in the fridge for up to 2 days.

MAKES 4–6 PORTIONS

Roasted pumpkin

600 g butternut pumpkin, peeled and cut into thick slices
1 tablespoon coconut oil or other good-quality fat*, melted
125 ml (½ cup) homemade beef stock (page 84) or water

Preheat the oven to 180°C. Place the pumpkin on a greased baking tray and drizzle with the coconut oil. Bake for 45–50 minutes, or until tender. Leave to cool. Mash the pumpkin with a fork or puree with a hand-held blender and mix with the stock or water. Store in an airtight container in the fridge for 2–3 days.

MAKES 6 PORTIONS

Apple, peach and berry

3 granny smith apples, peeled, cored and chopped
2 peaches, chopped
155 g (½ cup) fresh or frozen blueberries

Place the apple, peach, blueberries and 125 ml of water in a saucepan over medium–low heat and simmer until the apple and peach are tender and the blueberries have burst, 10–12 minutes. Set aside to cool. Transfer the apple mixture to a food processor and puree until smooth, adding more water, if necessary. Store in an airtight container in the fridge for up to 2 days.

MAKES 6 PORTIONS

* See Glossary

Beef and vegetable

2 teaspoons coconut oil or other good-quality fat*

½ small onion, finely chopped

1 small garlic clove, crushed

1 celery stalk, finely chopped

1 small carrot, coarsely grated

½ parsnip, coarsely grated

150 g beef mince

4 tablespoons homemade beef stock (page 84) or water

* *See Glossary*

Heat the oil in a frying pan over medium–low heat. Add the onion, garlic and celery and cook, stirring, for 2–3 minutes until the onion softens. Stir in the carrot and parsnip and cook for 2–3 minutes until tender. Add the beef mince and cook, stirring with a wooden spoon to break up any lumps, for 5 minutes until the mince is browned and cooked all the way through. Pour in the stock and bring to the boil. Reduce the heat to low and cook for a further 10 minutes until the sauce thickens slightly. Place the mince mixture in a food processor and blend until almost smooth. Serve warm. Store in an airtight container in the fridge for 3–4 days.

MAKES 5–6 PORTIONS

Turmeric-spiced fish

1 tablespoon ghee*

1 small onion, finely chopped

1 garlic clove, finely chopped

1 tablespoon chopped mint leaves

pinch of ground cumin

2 pinches of ground turmeric or ½ teaspoon finely grated fresh turmeric

1 tomato, chopped

4 tablespoons homemade chicken or fish stock (pages 86 and 87) or water

260 g white fish fillet (such as whiting, snapper or perch – check very carefully for any bones), cubed

Cauliflower Rice (page 180)

* *See Glossary*

Melt the ghee in a frying pan over low heat. Add the onion, garlic and mint and sauté, stirring, until the onion is golden brown (about 10 minutes). Add the cumin and turmeric, stir and cook for a few more minutes. Stir in the tomato and continue to cook until the tomato is cooked to a pulp. Pour in the stock or water, add the fish, ensuring it is covered by the sauce, and simmer for about 10 minutes until the fish is cooked. Serve with some cauliflower rice mixed through. Store in an airtight container in the fridge for 2–3 days.

MAKES 4 PORTIONS

Lamb, mushroom and bone marrow

Whiting, broccoli and carrot

Turmeric-spiced fish

Chicken and vegetable

Beef and vegetable

Beef, pumpkin and tomato

Beef, pumpkin and tomato

2 Roma tomatoes

1 teaspoon coconut oil or other good-quality fat*

120 g beef mince

350 g butternut pumpkin, peeled and diced

150 g (about ¼ head) broccoli, broken into florets

170 ml (⅔ cup) homemade beef stock (page 84) or water

* See Glossary

Cut a small cross in the top of each tomato. Transfer to a heatproof bowl, cover with freshly boiled water and let stand for 30 seconds. Drain the tomatoes and plunge them into cold water. Peel off the skins. Cut the skinned tomatoes into quarters, scoop out the seeds, and chop the flesh. Heat the oil or fat in a large frying pan over medium heat. Add the beef and cook, stirring to break up any lumps, for 2–3 minutes, or until browned. Add the pumpkin, broccoli and tomato and sauté, stirring, for 2–5 minutes, or until the vegetables are softened. Add the stock and bring to the boil. Reduce the heat to low, cover and simmer for 15 minutes, or until the vegetables are tender. Place in a food processor and blend until smooth, adding a little extra boiled water or stock if the puree is too thick. Store in an airtight container in the fridge for 2–3 days.

MAKES 6 PORTIONS

Whiting, broccoli and carrot

2 carrots, sliced

4 broccoli florets (about 160 g in total), cut into small pieces

200 g whiting or other white fish fillet, skin and bones removed and flesh cut into strips

125 ml (½ cup) coconut milk

Place the carrot and broccoli in a steamer, cover and steam for 6–8 minutes, or until really tender. Meanwhile, place the fish and coconut milk in a small saucepan, cover and cook over medium heat for about 2 minutes, or until the fish flakes easily. Transfer the vegetable and fish mixture to a blender and puree until smooth. Add a little more coconut milk, if necessary. Transfer the puree to a glass bowl and set it in a second bowl of ice to cool quickly, then cover and refrigerate. To serve, heat in a small saucepan until hot, stirring occasionally and adding a little more milk if necessary. Cool to warm before serving. Store in an airtight container in the fridge for 2 days.

MAKES 6 PORTIONS

Chicken and vegetable

300 g sweet potato, peeled and cut into 1 cm cubes

1 turnip, peeled and cut into 1 cm cubes

1 carrot, peeled and sliced

1 tablespoon coconut oil or other good-quality fat*

1 small French shallot or ¼ small onion, finely chopped

140 g chicken mince

2 handfuls of baby spinach, washed

125 ml (½ cup) homemade chicken stock (page 86) or water

* See Glossary

Put the sweet potato, turnip and carrot in a steamer basket, cover and steam over a saucepan of simmering water until tender (about 10 minutes). Remove from the steamer and set aside. Meanwhile, melt the oil in a large frying pan over medium heat. Add the shallot or onion and chicken and stir-fry for 2–3 minutes, or until the chicken is browned and crumbly. Add the spinach and sauté for 1 minute, or until wilted. Add the cooked veggies and chicken broth, cover and simmer gently for 5 minutes, or until very tender. Place in a food processor and process to a puree. Thin with a little water, if necessary. Store in an airtight container in the fridge for 2–3 days.

MAKES 8 PORTIONS

Lamb, mushroom and bone marrow

2 tablespoons coconut oil or other good-quality fat*

300 g lean lamb shoulder, cubed

300 g beef marrow bones, cut into 5 cm pieces

1 large portobello mushroom, sliced

1 handful of green beans

2 carrots, chopped

250 ml (1 cup) homemade beef stock (page 84) or water

pinch of freshly ground black pepper

* See Glossary

Preheat the oven to 160°C. Melt the coconut oil in a non-stick frying pan over medium heat. Add the lamb and seal until brown on all sides (about 4 minutes). Meanwhile, pop out the marrow from the bones and slice the bone marrow into 5 mm thick pieces. Add to the lamb and fry until lightly brown – about 30 seconds on each side. Transfer the meat, marrow and pan juices to a small ovenproof dish, then add the mushroom, beans and carrot and pour over the beef stock. Season with pepper, cover the dish with foil or a lid and bake in the oven for 1½ hours until the meat is tender. If needed, add more liquid after an hour of cooking. Set aside to cool slightly. Roughly mash, chop or pulse the lamb and vegetables in a food processor and serve warm. Store in an airtight containerin the fridge for up to 3 days.

MAKES 8 PORTIONS

KIDS' LUNCHES

You can add anything you like to green goddess dressing, as long as the end result is green and creamy. The go-to staple ingredients are green herbs and avocado, to which you add some acid from vinegar or citrus fruit and some aromatic seasonings, such as fennel seeds, cumin seeds, sumac, ginger, garlic, green chillies or lemongrass. If you want to make it super nutritious, add some pau d'arco powder, slippery elm powder, licorice root or olive leaf extract. I love to serve green goddess with a multitude of dishes, from salads to fritters like these.

VEGGIE FRITTERS WITH GREEN GODDESS DRESSING

500 g zucchini, grated

250 g sweet potato, grated

1 carrot, grated

¼ fennel bulb (about 50 g), shaved

generous pinch of Himalayan salt

1 handful of flat-leaf parsley leaves, chopped

1 handful of mint leaves, chopped

3 spring onions, finely chopped

zest of 1 lemon

3 eggs

50 g (½ cup) almond meal

freshly ground black pepper

4 tablespoons coconut oil

rocket leaves, to serve (optional)

lemon wedges, to serve (optional)

GREEN GODDESS DRESSING

½ avocado

3 tablespoons coconut milk

3 tablespoons lemon juice

1 garlic clove, finely chopped

2 anchovy fillets, finely chopped

½ cup chopped flat-leaf parsley leaves

3 tablespoons chopped basil leaves

1 tablespoon chopped tarragon leaves

¼ teaspoon sea salt

125 ml (½ cup) extra-virgin olive oil

Place the zucchini, sweet potato, carrot and fennel in a colander over a bowl. Sprinkle on the salt and mix well. Leave the salted vegetables to sit for 15 minutes until they begin to sweat.

Meanwhile, make the green goddess dressing. Place all the ingredients except the oil in a food processor or blender and process until well combined. With the motor running, slowly pour in the oil and process until the dressing thickens and the herbs are finely chopped. Transfer to a bowl and refrigerate until ready to serve.

Use your hands to squeeze out the excess moisture from the vegetables. Make sure you remove as much liquid as possible, otherwise the fritters will be soggy.

Place the zucchini, sweet potato, carrot and fennel in a large bowl. Add the parsley, mint, spring onion, lemon zest, eggs, almond meal and a pinch of pepper and mix well.

At this stage, test the fritter mixture to check it is binding properly by forming a small amount into a ball and frying it with a little oil in a non-stick frying pan. If the fritter tends to break apart easily, add a little more almond meal and mix thoroughly.

Divide and shape the mixture into small, evenly sized, lightly flattened patties. Melt the ghee or coconut oil in a non-stick frying pan over medium heat and fry the fritters in batches for 2 minutes on each side, or until cooked through. Drain on paper towel.

Serve the fritters warm with the goddess dressing, rocket leaves and lemon wedges, if desired, or chill and serve as a lunchbox meal. Any leftover dressing can be stored in an airtight container in the fridge for up to 5 days.

SERVES 4–6

So many French dishes translate well to a paleo way of life. As I write this, I have some duck legs slowly cooking in their own fat for breakfast tomorrow. One of my favourite French dishes is the classic salade Niçoise. The original version includes potatoes and green beans. I've swapped the starchy potatoes for Jerusalem artichokes and used asparagus as well as green beans as I just adore it. Magnifique!

TUNA NIÇOISE SALAD

400 g Jerusalem artichokes, peeled and sliced into 2.5 cm pieces

2 tablespoons coconut oil or other good-quality fat*, melted

salt and freshly ground black pepper

6 eggs

1 bunch of asparagus spears, trimmed and cut into 5 cm lengths

200 g green beans, halved

250 g teardrop or cherry tomatoes, halved

150 g (1 cup) pitted Niçoise olives (or other black olives)

8 white anchovy fillets (optional)

8 caperberries, halved

1 red onion, finely sliced

2 baby cos lettuces, trimmed, cut into quarters and leaves separated

400 g good-quality canned tuna in brine or olive oil, liquid drained

VINAIGRETTE

1 garlic clove, crushed

1 teaspoon Dijon mustard

3 tablespoons apple cider vinegar

juice of ½ lemon

2 tablespoons chopped flat-leaf parsley leaves

2 tablespoons chopped tarragon leaves

125 ml (½ cup) extra-virgin olive oil

* See Glossary

To make the vinaigrette, combine all the ingredients in a bowl and whisk well. Set aside while preparing the salad.

Preheat the oven to 200°C. Line a baking tray with baking paper.

Scatter the Jerusalem artichokes on the tray in a single layer, drizzle on the coconut oil and season with salt and pepper. Roast in the oven for 8–10 minutes, stirring and tossing the artichoke after 4–5 minutes, until lightly golden and cooked through.

Place the eggs in a large saucepan of water. Bring to the boil over medium heat and simmer for 5 minutes, or until cooked to your liking.

Meanwhile, place the asparagus and beans in a steamer basket or colander and put on top of the pan containing the simmering eggs. Cover and steam the asparagus and beans for 2–3 minutes until tender but still crisp. Remove from the heat, plunge the asparagus and beans into iced water, then drain well. Peel the eggs in cold running water and set aside.

To assemble the salad, combine the Jerusalem artichoke, asparagus, beans, tomatoes, olives, anchovies (if using), capers, onion and lettuce leaves in a large bowl. Season with salt and pepper. Add just enough dressing to moisten the ingredients, then toss gently to coat.

Arrange the salad on a serving platter or individual plates. Place the tuna and quartered eggs on top. Drizzle with the remaining vinaigrette and serve.

SERVES 4

I love the creativity that comes with cooking. This is a simple but exciting dish that I created as an alternative to using sushi rice. I took some leftover cauliflower rice, added nut butter for creaminess and tahini to give some extra stickiness. Have a play around with different fillings and dipping sauces. There are no rules to eating this way.

TUNA AND AVOCADO SUSHI ROLLS

2 cups Cauliflower Rice (page 180)

2 tablespoons tahini

3 tablespoons cashew or macadamia nut butter

sea salt

1 × 150 g can of good-quality tuna in olive oil or brine, drained

2 tablespoons mayonnaise (to make your own, see page 58), plus extra to serve

2 pinches of chilli powder (optional)

4 toasted nori sheets*

1 large handful of rocket leaves

1 cucumber, sliced lengthways into eighths and seeds removed

½ carrot, sliced into thin batons

½ avocado, sliced into strips

toasted white and black sesame seeds, to serve

tamari, to serve

wasabi, to serve

See Glossary

Combine the cauliflower rice, tahini and cashew or macadamia nut butter in a bowl, season with salt and mix well

In another bowl, mix the tuna, mayonnaise and chilli (if using).

Place a nori sheet on a bench (or a bamboo sushi mat, if using). Spread one-quarter of the cauliflower rice mix on half of the nori sheet, working from the edge closest to you and spreading it right to the sides. Layer the tuna, rocket, cucumber, carrot and avocado across the middle of the cauliflower rice and, starting with the edge closest to you, begin to tightly wrap the roll all the way to the end. Trim the ends with a sharp knife, then cut into 2 cm round pieces. Repeat with the remaining nori, cauliflower rice and fillings.

Place the sushi pieces on a platter and sprinkle over some sesame seeds. Serve with mayonnaise, tamari and wasabi.

MAKES 32 PIECES

This is a fun little take on the old ham and salad sanga. I've used lettuce as the wraps, but feel free to use coconut tortillas (page 141), buckwheat crepes or paleo bread (pages 23 and 24) for a true sandwich. Please source the best quality pastured ham you can spend your hard-earned cash on. If you avoid pork, replace it with cooked chook, prawns, tuna or salmon. Or simply chop up all the ingredients with some avo to make a killer salad!

HAM, EGG AND MAYO LETTUCE WRAPS

2 hard-boiled eggs, chopped

2 tablespoons mayonnaise (to make your own, see recipe below)

sea salt and freshly ground black pepper

2 large cos lettuce leaves

4 thin slices of ham

1 carrot, grated

1 Lebanese cucumber, sliced

1 beetroot, peeled and grated (wear gloves!)

MAYONNAISE

1 egg

2 egg yolks

1 teaspoon Dijon mustard

½ teaspoon fine sea salt

1 tablespoon apple cider vinegar

1 tablespoon lemon juice

500 ml light olive oil or macadamia oil

Mix the egg and 2 tablespoons of the mayonnaise until well combined; season with salt and pepper.

Place two sheets of baking paper on a workbench or chopping board and put a lettuce leaf on each sheet. Equally divide the ham, carrot, cucumber, beetroot and egg mayo between the lettuce leaves, then roll up, wrap tightly and cut in half.

MAYONNAISE

To make your own mayonnaise, place the egg, egg yolks, mustard, salt, vinegar and lemon juice in a food processor and process for 1–2 minutes, or until nice and smooth. With the motor running, slowly pour in the oil and process until it has emulsified and become thick and creamy. Season with a little more salt if needed. Leftover mayo can be stored in an airtight container in the fridge for up to 4 days.

SERVES 2

TIP

If your kids love curried eggs, simply mix 1 teaspoon of curry powder into the eggs and mayo.

This is my favourite photo in the book. I won't say it is my favourite recipe because that is way too hard to pick! When I look at this image, I just want to eat this salad – for breakfast, lunch or dinner – because, seriously, that is when this dish should and can be eaten. It makes the most gorgeous breakfast – it is basically bacon and eggs with some greens, which is one of my favourite ways to start the day. It is also the perfect lunch to take to work or school (the pine nuts might be an issue at some schools), as it is filling and nutritious. And for dinner . . . well, it is perfect, as it isn't too heavy and it's something that can be whipped up in under 15 minutes. Now, when you look at this photo, does it say the same thing?

KALE CAESAR SALAD

6–8 rashers of bacon

4 eggs

1 bunch (about 300 g) of kale, thinly sliced

juice of 1 lemon

3 teaspoons extra-virgin olive oil

2 tablespoons chopped flat-leaf parsley leaves

4 tablespoons pine nuts, toasted

4 anchovy fillets, rinsed and halved (optional)

4 macadamia nuts, grated

CAESAR DRESSING

2 egg yolks

4 anchovy fillets, rinsed and finely chopped

½ garlic clove, crushed

1 tablespoon lemon juice

1 teaspoon Dijon mustard

250 ml (1 cup) light olive oil

sea salt and freshly ground black pepper

Pan-fry the bacon until crisp and golden. Remove from the pan, drain on paper towel and leave to cool. Chop into small pieces and set aside.

Place the eggs in a large saucepan of water. Bring to the boil over medium heat and simmer for 5 minutes, or until cooked to your liking. Remove from the heat, drain and cool in iced water. Peel, quarter and set aside.

To make the caesar dressing, combine the egg yolks, anchovies, garlic, lemon juice and mustard in a food processor or blender. Process briefly until combined. With the motor running, gradually add the oil, drop by drop, until the dressing has emulsified and thickened slightly. Now pour in the oil in a steady stream and continue to process until the dressing is the consistency of pouring cream. Check the seasoning, adding salt and pepper or more lemon juice as desired.

Place the kale in a bowl and add the lemon juice and olive oil. Mix gently, rubbing the lemon juice and oil into the kale, and allow to stand for 5 minutes.

Place half the caesar dressing on the kale and mix gently.

Tip the dressed kale into a large serving bowl and scatter on the parsley, pine nuts and anchovies (if using). Top the salad with the bacon, soft-boiled eggs and grated macadamia nuts.

SERVES 4

In another lifetime, I used to make pizzas for a living. In fact, my pizzas went on to win national and international awards. This kid-friendly recipe is free of gluten, yeast and dairy, but is still crispy and delicious. The topping that looks like cheese is actually grated macadamia nuts. I make this from time to time for the girls in my house – Indii, Chilli and Nic – and they love it.

HAM AND PINEAPPLE MINI PIZZAS

1 Paleo Pizza Base (page 91)

½ pineapple, top removed, peeled and cored (about 200 g pineapple flesh)

2 tablespoons chopped flat-leaf parsley

12–16 cherry tomatoes, sliced

200 g Cashew Cheese (page 218)

200 g leg ham, cut into 5 mm thick slices

sea salt and freshly ground black pepper

4 macadamia nuts, grated

basil leaves, torn, to serve

extra-virgin olive oil, to serve

PIZZA SAUCE

1 × 400 g can whole peeled tomatoes

¼ teaspoon Himalayan salt or sea salt

1 teaspoon dried oregano

2 pinches of freshly ground black pepper

To make your paleo pizza base follow the instructions on page 91. When it comes time to spread the dough out on the tray, spread it into four 15 cm circles. Continue to follow the instructions on page 91, until you have precooked the bases in the oven until lightly golden.

Reduce the oven to 160°C.

Place the pineapple on a baking tray and roast for 8 minutes until lightly golden. Set aside to cool, then cut into 3 mm thick slices.

To make the pizza sauce, combine all the ingredients in a food processor and process until smooth.

Increase the oven temperature to 240°C or the highest temperature setting. If you have a pizza stone, place it in the oven to heat up for 15 minutes. If you don't, you can use a baking tray, which does not require preheating.

Spread 2 tablespoons of the pizza sauce evenly over each of the four partly cooked bases. Scatter over the parsley, cherry tomatoes, cashew cheese, ham and pineapple. Season with salt and pepper.

Transfer the pizzas to the heated pizza stone (or simply leave them on the baking tray if you don't have a pizza stone). Bake in the oven for 5–10 minutes, or until golden and crispy. Sprinkle on the grated macadamia and basil leaves and drizzle with olive oil. Cut into wedges to serve. Leftover pizza sauce can be stored in an airtight container in the fridge for up to 1 week or in the freezer for up to 3 months.

SERVES 4

Pad Thai was my first introduction to Thai food. I absolutely adore the fragrance, the taste and the texture. With this recipe all I have done is substitute the rice noodles with kelp noodles. You could use zucchini noodles (page 88) or parsnip noodles (page 154) if you prefer and swap the peanuts for some macadamias, cashews or Brazil nuts. I hope you enjoy this paleo version of one of my all-time favourite dishes.

PAD THAI

250 g kelp noodles*

3 tablespoons honey (optional)

2 tablespoons tamarind* paste

1 teaspoon apple cider vinegar

1 tablespoon fish sauce

2 tablespoons coconut oil

2 red Asian shallots, thinly sliced

2 garlic cloves, crushed

1 long red chilli, deseeded and finely chopped (optional)

1 chicken thigh fillet, cut into strips

1 tablespoon dried shrimp

3 tablespoons chopped raw cashews, plus extra to serve

2 eggs

1 handful of beans sprouts, plus extra to serve

1 small handful of garlic chives, cut into 2.5 cm batons

lime wedges, to serve

See Glossary

Rinse the noodles in cold water. Bring a saucepan filled with water to the boil. Add the noodles, blanch for 2 minutes, drain and set aside.

Mix the honey (if using) with the tamarind, vinegar, fish sauce and 2 tablespoons of water in a bowl and stir until well combined.

Heat the coconut oil in a wok or large, deep frying pan over medium–high heat. Add the shallot and fry for 1–2 minutes, stirring continuously, until fragrant and a light golden colour. Add the garlic and chilli (if using) and stir-fry for a few seconds, then add the chicken and cook, tossing constantly, for 15 seconds. Stir in the kelp noodles and fry for about 30 seconds. Pour in the honey mixture and simmer until almost absorbed. Mix in the dried shrimp and cashews, add a splash of water and cook, tossing, for a further minute.

Push the noodle mixture to one side of the wok or pan and crack in the eggs on the other side. Lightly scramble the eggs for 20 seconds, or until cooked, then toss the noodle mixture with the eggs. Add the bean sprouts and garlic chives and stir-fry for another minute, or until the sprouts and chives are heated through. Check for seasoning.

Divide between two plates, sprinkle with the extra bean sprouts and cashews and serve with the lime wedges.

SERVES 2

Why would I have a chicken nugget recipe in this book, you might ask. Well, they can be healthy. All you need is topnotch ingredients. Try to source organic, free-range chicken. I find the best parts for nuggets are the tenderloins, those little fillets attached to the breasts. If using the whole breast, cut on the diagonal and make sure you don't overcook it. You can also use thigh meat – just make sure you cut it into uniform pieces, so that it cooks evenly. Instead of breadcrumbs, this recipe uses almond meal and arrowroot. You can vary the texture by adding shredded coconut or sesame seeds, or even make your own paleo breadcrumbs by drying a couple of slices of paleo bread (page 23 and 24) in the oven and then blitzing them up.

CHICKEN NUGGETS

2 chicken breast fillets

2 eggs

60 ml (¼ cup) coconut milk

150 g (1½ cups) almond meal

125 g (1 cup) arrowroot*

½ teaspoon garlic powder

½ teaspoon onion powder

1 teaspoon Himalayan salt

½ teaspoon freshly ground black pepper

250 ml (1 cup) coconut oil or other good-quality fat*

good-quality tomato ketchup (to make your own, see page 72), to serve

* See Glossary

Remove the tenderloin from the chicken breasts and use a meat mallet to gently pound out the tenderloins and breasts so they are all about 2 cm thick. Using a sharp knife, chop the chicken into 5-cm long pieces. Pat dry using paper towel.

Break the eggs into a bowl and whisk with the coconut milk until well combined.

In another bowl, place the almond meal, half of the arrowroot, the garlic, onion powder, salt and pepper. Mix well then set aside.

Place the remaining arrowroot in a separate bowl.

Individually coat each chicken piece in the arrowroot, shaking off any excess. Next, dip each piece in the egg mixture and roll in the almond meal crumbs, making sure the pieces are coated evenly. If there are any areas that remain uncoated, simply dab a little more egg mixture onto the dry areas and coat again with the almond meal crumbs.

Heat the oil or fat in a large, deep frying pan over medium heat. Test the heat of the oil or fat by placing a small piece of chicken in the pan. When the fat or oil begins to sizzle around the chicken, it has reached its ideal heat. Add the chicken nuggets, in batches, and cook for 3 minutes on each side, or until golden brown and the chicken is cooked through. Remove the nuggets from the pan using metal tongs or a slotted spoon, and drain on paper towel. Allow the nuggets to cool for 2 minutes before serving with tomato ketchup.

SERVES 4

Has there ever been a more family-oriented dish than the classic san choy bau? I like to start with aromatics such as garlic, ginger, coriander root, spring onion and tamari as the foundation, and then play around with different proteins (minced pork, lamb, beef, chicken, duck, quail, prawn, lobster, crab or bug meat or any combination of these) that I mix with water chestnuts and mushrooms. Feel free to add bean sprouts, loads of herbs, sesame seeds, grated zucchini, carrot, water spinach, kale, cauliflower, asparagus, okra . . . This is how you create recipes, with an open mind and palate.

CHICKEN SAN CHOY BAU

1 tablespoon coconut oil

3 garlic cloves, crushed

4 spring onions, finely chopped

2 teaspoons finely grated ginger

600 g chicken mince

120 g shiitake mushrooms, chopped

1 tablespoon fish sauce

1 teaspoon honey (optional)

2 tablespoons tamari

200 g water chestnuts, drained and finely chopped

1–2 long red chillies, deseeded and chopped (optional)

100 g bean sprouts

sea salt and freshly ground black pepper

6 large iceberg lettuce leaves, washed and dried

1 handful of coriander leaves

1 lime, quartered

Heat a wok or large frying pan over medium–high heat. Add the coconut oil, garlic, spring onion and ginger and cook for 1 minute. Stir in the chicken mince and mushrooms and cook for 4–5 minutes, stirring occasionally to break up any lumps, until brown and cooked through.

Toss the fish sauce, honey (if using) and tamari through the mince, then add the water chestnuts and chilli (if using), stirring until well combined. Cook for 2–3 minutes until heated through.

Remove the pan from the heat, mix in the bean sprouts and season to taste, adding more fish sauce if required.

Place the lettuce cups on a serving platter or on individual plates and spoon in some of the chicken mixture. Garnish with the coriander leaves and a squeeze of lime and serve.

SERVES 6

I urge you to get the kids involved (no matter how old they are) when making these meatballs. Kids love to learn, they love attention and they love to feel they have accomplished something. It is great to see them do their best and to see them eat these meatballs without hesitation. Never underestimate children when it comes to trying new things, including ingredients you never thought they would eat.

LAMB KOFTA WITH KALE AND TAHINI DIP

500 g lamb mince

1 garlic clove, crushed

½ onion, finely chopped

1 teaspoon dried mint

3 tablespoons chopped flat-leaf parsley leaves

1 tablespoon lemon juice

1 teaspoon sea salt

¼ teaspoon freshly ground black pepper

coconut oil, for frying

salad, to serve

Kale and Tahini Dip (page 219), to serve

Place the mince, garlic, onion, mint, parsley, lemon juice and salt and pepper in a large bowl and mix by hand until well combined. Using wet hands, evenly divide the kofta mixture into 10 balls and shape them into patties.

Heat a barbecue hotplate or large frying pan to medium and add a little coconut oil.

Cook the kofta, turning occasionally, for 8–10 minutes, or until cooked through.

Serve while hot with a salad and the kale and tahini dip.

SERVES 4

Looking at this image I immediately think it is a regular hotdog with a bun. In fact, I have substituted the bun for a slow-roasted sweet potato and topped it with a delicious gourmet wheat-free sausage that you can make yourself or pick up from a quality butcher or health food store. These are super easy to make and will be a hit at your next kids' party. I like to serve some kraut (page 178) or a little garden salad (page 168) on the side.

HOT DOGS WITH A SWEET POTATO BUN

2 sweet potatoes, unpeeled (try to pick out straight ones if possible)

1½ teaspoons sesame seeds

1 tablespoon coconut oil or other good-quality fat *

2 gourmet sausages of your choice

Cultured Tomato Ketchup (see below), to serve

Dijon mustard or Fermented Mustard (page 177), to serve

CULTURED TOMATO KETCHUP

500 g good-quality or homemade tomato paste

3 tablespoons honey or maple syrup (optional)

½ sachet vegetable starter culture *

2 tablespoons lemon juice, plus extra to thin

1 teaspoon sea salt

freshly ground black pepper

1 garlic clove, finely chopped

1 long red chilli, deseeded and finely chopped

1 teaspoon ground allspice

½ teaspoon ground cloves

See Glossary

Preheat the oven to 100°C.

Place the sweet potatoes on a baking tray and roast for about 6 hours, or until very tender.

Cut the sweet potatoes almost in half lengthways. Do not cut all the way through. Slightly open up the cut centre part, then carefully peel away the skin, sprinkle with the sesame seeds and set aside.

Meanwhile, heat the oil or fat in a large frying pan over medium–high heat. Add the sausages and reduce the heat to medium. Cook, turning occasionally, for 8–10 minutes, or until cooked through.

Place the sausages lengthways in the centre cut part of the sweet potato. Squeeze over some ketchup and mustard and serve.

CULTURED TOMATO KETCHUP

To make your own cultured tomato ketchup, you'll need a 750 ml preserving jar with an airlock lid. Wash the jar and utensils in very hot water or run them through a hot rinse cycle on the dishwasher.

Place the tomato paste in a large bowl and fold through the honey or maple syrup (if using). Whisk in the vegetable starter culture along with 120 ml of water, the lemon juice, salt, a few grinds of pepper, garlic, chilli, allspice and cloves. Whisk until smooth. Add some extra lemon juice if you'd like a thinner sauce. Spoon into the preserving jar and close the lid. Wrap a tea towel around the side of the jar to block out the light.

Store the jar in a dark place with a temperature of 16–23°C for 3–5 days. The warmer the weather the shorter the amount of time needed. The longer you leave the jar, the higher the level of good bacteria present and the tangier the flavour. Give the ketchup a good stir before transferring to the fridge, where it will keep for several months.

SERVES 2

You haven't just been transported to a parallel universe; this is the real deal and one that will redefine pizza nights in your household. Next time you have a sleepover at your house and you don't know what to cook, just remember the meatzza and get the kids to spice their meat base and then top it with whatever they choose. The best way is to lay out all the ingredients and show them what to do. This is much easier to clean up and quicker and easier to make than a traditional doughy pizza base, and it will fill them up and sustain them for a lot longer, too, which earns a huge tick in my book.

MEATZZA

BASE
200 g beef mince

200 g pork mince

1 egg yolk

¼ onion, finely diced

1 garlic clove, crushed

1 tablespoon finely chopped flat-leaf parsley leaves

½ teaspoon dried oregano

¾ teaspoon sea salt

¼ teaspoon freshly ground black pepper

TOPPING
4 tablespoons Pizza Sauce (page 63)

8 kalamata olives, pitted

8 cherry tomatoes, halved

60 g Macadamia Cheese (page 218)

leaves of 1 rosemary sprig or 6 basil leaves, roughly chopped

Preheat the oven to 250°C or the highest temperature setting.

To make the base, place all the ingredients in a bowl and knead until well combined.

Grease a 30 cm pizza tray with a little oil and line with baking paper.

Place the beef mixture on the pizza tray and use your hands to flatten it evenly to cover the tray. Bake for 6–8 minutes until the meat is cooked through. Remove and drain any excess liquid from the tray.

Spread the pizza sauce evenly over the base. Add the olives, cherry tomatoes, macadamia cheese and season with salt and pepper.

Return the meatzza to the oven and cook for a further 5–10 minutes, or until lightly brown.

Use the paper to carefully transfer the meatzza to a chopping board or plate. Cut into wedges, then scatter on some rosemary or basil and serve.

SERVES 2–3

As a young boy, one of my favourite things to eat at birthday parties was party pies. The party pies came from the frozen section in the supermarket, were smothered with sugar-laden tomato sauce and were usually served alongside some cocktail frankfurts. I think it's important for kids to still have treats – especially on their birthday – so I have created this paleo party pie recipe for you to try making for their next party. Just because we are looking after our health it doesn't mean we have to miss out on party pies!

PARTY PIES

2 tablespoons ghee*

1 large onion, finely chopped

2 large garlic cloves, crushed

1 carrot, finely chopped

2 large portobello mushrooms, chopped

500 g beef mince

100 g beef liver, finely chopped

1 tablespoon tomato paste

1 tablespoon tapioca flour* mixed with 2 tablespoons cold water

375 ml (1½ cups) beef stock (to make your own, see page 84)

1 tablespoon coconut aminos* or tamari

2 teaspoons chopped thyme leaves

2 bay leaves

sea salt and freshly ground black pepper

800 g Short Pastry (page 147)

1 egg

2 tablespoons coconut milk or almond milk

good-quality tomato ketchup (to make your own, see page 72), to serve

* See Glossary

To make the short pastry, follow the instructions on page 147.

While the short pastry dough is resting for 30 minutes in the fridge, melt the ghee in a large frying pan over medium heat. Add the onion, garlic and carrot and cook for 2–4 minutes until the carrot softens. Stir in the mushrooms and cook for a further 2 minutes. Add the mince and liver and cook, stirring, for 6–8 minutes until brown. Stir in the tomato paste and the tapioca flour mixture and cook for a further minute. Add the stock, coconut aminos, thyme and bay leaves and season with salt and pepper. Bring to the boil, reduce the heat to low and simmer, stirring occasionally, for 15–20 minutes until thickened and most of the liquid has evaporated. Remove from the heat and set aside. Remove the bay leaves once cool.

Preheat the oven to 180°C. Grease two 8-hole muffin tins.

Roll out the pastry to 5 mm thick on a lightly floured work surface. Using a 6.5 cm round cutter, cut out 16 discs and line the muffin tins. Place the muffin tins in the oven to bake for about 6 minutes, or until the bases are just starting to colour. Allow to cool.

Spoon 1½ tablespoons of filling into each pastry case and pat down with the back of the spoon. Reroll the remaining pastry between sheets of baking paper to 8 mm thick. To make the lids, cut out 16 rounds with a 6 cm cutter. Pierce holes in the centre of each round with a floured fork, place one on top of each pastry case and press the edges together to seal. If the pastry becomes difficult to handle, place it in the fridge for 10 minutes to firm up.

To make the egg wash, whisk together the egg and coconut milk or almond milk for a few seconds, then season with a little salt. Reduce the oven to 160°C. Brush the top of each pie with the egg wash and bake for 15–20 minutes until golden. Turn the tins around after 10 minutes to ensure the pies brown evenly. Stand for 2 minutes before removing from the tins. Serve with tomato ketchup.

MAKES 16

I have so many meatball recipes and I reckon I make them almost weekly for my family. Not only are meatballs cheap, they are delicious and the kids love making them, too. I have used vegetable noodles here as a fun way to incorporate more veggies in the kids' diet, and I find this works a treat. If you don't have success with vegetable noodles, try kelp noodles or simply grate the veggies into the meatballs and serve them without noodles. I find if you get the kids involved in making the noodles, they will be tempted to give them a twirl!

SPAGHETTI AND MEATBALLS

4 tablespoons coconut oil or ghee*

2 handfuls of baby spinach leaves

1 French shallot, finely chopped

2 garlic cloves, finely chopped

350 g pork mince

150 g beef mince

2 tablespoons finely chopped flat-leaf parsley leaves

1 egg yolk

Himalayan salt or sea salt and freshly ground black pepper

1 large handful of flat-leaf parsley or basil leaves, finely chopped, to serve

TOMATO SAUCE

2 tablespoons coconut oil or ghee*

2 garlic cloves, thinly sliced

500 g (2 cups) canned crushed tomatoes

8 basil leaves, chopped

VEGETABLE SPAGHETTI

3 large carrots, cut into spaghetti strips on a mandoline or slicer

6 zucchinis, cut into spaghetti strips on a mandoline or slicer

2 tablespoons extra-virgin olive oil

* See Glossary

To make the meatballs, melt 1 tablespoon of the ghee or coconut oil in a frying pan over medium heat. Add the spinach and cook for 2 minutes until just wilted. Drain the spinach and leave to cool. Once cool, squeeze out any excess liquid, roughly chop and transfer to a bowl.

Return the pan to medium heat and add 1 tablespoon of the coconut oil or ghee, the shallot and garlic. Fry for 3 minutes, or until the shallot is translucent and the garlic is lightly browned. Set aside.

In a large bowl, mix the pork mince, beef mince, spinach, shallot and garlic, parsley, egg yolk and some salt and pepper until well combined. Roll into golf ball-sized portions and set aside.

Preheat the oven to 180°C.

To make the tomato sauce, heat the coconut oil or ghee in a saucepan over medium heat. Add the garlic and fry for 30 seconds, or until lightly browned. Pour in the tomatoes and 125 ml of water, then simmer for 20–25 minutes until the sauce has thickened. Add the basil and simmer for a further 2 minutes. Season with salt and pepper. You can blend the sauce if your kids prefer it smooth.

To cook the meatballs, heat the remaining 2 tablespoons of coconut oil or ghee in a large ovenproof frying pan. Add the meatballs and fry until golden on one side. Turn the meatballs over and place the pan in the oven for 5 minutes until the meatballs are cooked through. Remove the pan from the oven, add the tomato sauce, cover and keep warm.

To make the vegetable spaghetti, fill a saucepan with water and bring to the boil over medium heat. Add the carrot and cook for 30 seconds, then add the zucchini and cook for a further 30 seconds, or until tender. Drain, toss with a splash of the olive oil and season with salt.

Divide the spaghetti between four serving plates, top with the meatballs, spoon on the tomato sauce, sprinkle with the parsley or basil and serve.

SERVES 4

If you are looking for something quick, cheap, interesting and healthy to pop into your child's lunchbox, then look no further than these frittata muffins. They are packed with healthy fats and protein, and if you team them with some simple raw vegetables such as carrot, celery, cucumber, radishes or avocado, you've got a really healthy and delicious lunch. You can make these the night before and keep them in the fridge. They make an awesome breakfast, too.

PROSCIUTTO-WRAPPED FRITTATA MUFFINS

2 tablespoons coconut oil or other good-quality fat*, plus extra for greasing

½ onion, finely chopped

2 garlic cloves, crushed

6 Swiss brown mushrooms, thinly sliced

¼ red capsicum, finely chopped

1 tablespoon chopped flat-leaf parsley leaves

1 large handful of baby spinach leaves, roughly chopped

Himalayan salt and freshly ground black pepper

10 eggs

3 tablespoons nut milk (to make your own, see page 258) or coconut milk

2 tablespoons coconut flour

12 slices of prosciutto

8 cherry tomatoes, cut into 5 mm thick slices

Simple Garden Salad (page 168), to serve

*See Glossary

Preheat the oven to 175°C. Grease a 12-hole muffin tin with a little coconut oil.

Melt the coconut oil or fat in a large frying pan over medium heat. Add the onion and garlic and sauté for 2 minutes. Stir in the mushrooms and capsicum and sauté for a further 3 minutes, or until tender. Add the parsley and spinach and cook until the spinach is just wilted. Season with salt and pepper and transfer the cooked vegetables to a colander to drain off the excess liquid.

Crack the eggs into a large bowl and whisk with the nut or coconut milk and coconut flour. Season with salt and pepper, add the cooked vegetables and mix until well combined.

Line each muffin hole with 1 slice of prosciutto, covering the base and sides completely. Spoon in the frittata mixture until level with the rim of the tin. Top each muffin with 2 slices of cherry tomato.

Place the muffin tin in the oven and bake for 15–20 minutes, or until the muffins have risen and a metal skewer inserted in the centre of a muffin comes out clean and dry. Remove from the oven and allow the muffins to cool in the tin for 2 minutes before turning out onto a wire rack to cool completely. Serve hot with a garden salad, or chill and use for school lunches. Store in an airtight container in the fridge for 2 days.

MAKES 12

MAIN MEALS

BEEF STOCK

2 kg beef knuckle and marrow bones

1 calf's foot, cut into pieces (optional)

3 tablespoons apple cider vinegar

1.5 kg meaty rib or neck bones

3 onions, roughly chopped

3 carrots, roughly chopped

3 celery stalks, roughly chopped

2 leeks, white part only, rinsed and roughly chopped

several thyme sprigs, tied together

1 teaspoon black peppercorns, crushed

1 garlic bulb, halved across the cloves

2 large handfuls of flat-leaf parsley stalks

Place the knuckle and marrow bones and calf's foot (if using) in a stockpot or very large saucepan. Add the vinegar and pour in 4 litres of cold water, or enough to cover. Let stand for 1 hour.

Preheat the oven to 190°C.

Meanwhile, place the meaty bones in a roasting tin and roast for 30 minutes, or until well browned. Add the meaty bones to the stockpot along with the vegetables.

Transfer the fat from the roasting tin to a saucepan. Add 1 litre of water, place over high heat and bring to a simmer, stirring with a wooden spoon to loosen any coagulated juices. Add this liquid to the bones and vegetables. Add additional water, if necessary, to cover the bones and vegetables; but the liquid should come no higher than within 2 cm of the rim of the pan, as the volume expands slightly during cooking.

Bring the stock to the boil, skimming off the scum that rises to the top. Reduce the heat to low and add the thyme, peppercorns and garlic.

Simmer the stock for at least 8 hours. The longer you cook the stock the richer and more flavourful it will be. Just before finishing, add the parsley and simmer for another 10 minutes.

Strain the stock into a large container. Cover and cool in the fridge. Remove and discard the congealed fat that rises to the top. Transfer the stock to smaller airtight containers and place in the fridge or, for long-term storage, the freezer.

The stock will keep for 2–4 days in the fridge or up to 3 months in the freezer.

MAKES ABOUT 4 LITRES

CHICKEN STOCK

1–1.5 kg bony chicken parts
(such as necks, backs, breastbones
and wings)

2–4 chicken feet (optional)

2 tablespoons apple cider vinegar

1 large onion, roughly chopped

2 carrots, roughly chopped

3 celery stalks, roughly chopped

2 leeks, white part only, rinsed and
roughly chopped

1 garlic bulb, halved across the
cloves

1 tablespoon black peppercorns,
lightly crushed

2 large handfuls of flat-leaf
parsley stalks

Place the chicken pieces and feet (if using) in a stockpot or large saucepan and cover with 4 litres of cold water. Add the vinegar, onion, carrots, celery, leek, garlic and peppercorns and allow to stand for 30 minutes to 1 hour.

Place the pot over medium–high heat and bring to the boil, skimming off any scum that forms on the surface of the liquid. Reduce the heat to low and simmer for 6–8 hours, or until the meat has completely fallen off the bone. The longer you cook the stock the richer and more flavourful it will be. About 10 minutes before the stock is ready, add the parsley.

Strain the stock through a fine sieve into a large storage container, cover and place in the fridge until the fat rises to the top and congeals. Remove and discard this fat and reserve the stock in covered containers in the fridge or freezer. The stock will keep for 3–4 days in the fridge or 2–3 months in the freezer.

MAKES ABOUT 3.5 LITRES

FISH STOCK

2 tablespoons coconut oil

2 onions, roughly chopped

1 carrot, roughly chopped

125 ml (½ cup) dry white wine or vermouth (optional)

3–4 whole, non-oily fish carcasses (such as snapper, barramundi or kingfish), including heads

3 tablespoons apple cider vinegar

several thyme sprigs

several flat-leaf parsley stalks

1 dried bay leaf

Melt the oil in a stockpot or large saucepan over medium–low heat. Add the vegetables and cook very gently for about 30 minutes, or until soft. Pour in the wine or vermouth (if using) and bring to the boil. Add the fish carcasses and cover with 3 litres of cold water. Stir in the vinegar and bring to the boil, skimming off the scum that forms on the surface.

Tie the herbs together with kitchen string and add to the pot. Reduce the heat to low, cover and simmer for at least 2 hours.

Remove the carcasses with tongs or a slotted spoon and strain the liquid into storage containers for the fridge or freezer. Chill well in the fridge and remove any congealed fat before transferring to the freezer. The stock will keep for 2–3 days in the fridge or 2 months in the freezer.

MAKES ABOUT 2.5 LITRES

VEGETABLE STOCK

1 tablespoon coconut oil

1 onion, roughly chopped

2 large carrots, roughly chopped

2 parsnips, roughly chopped

1 celery stalk, roughly chopped

½ large bunch of silverbeet (about 600 g), chopped into 2.5 cm pieces

several thyme sprigs

several flat-leaf parsley stalks

1 dried bay leaf

In a stockpot or large saucepan, melt the coconut oil over medium–high heat. Add the onion and cook, stirring, for about 8 minutes, or until caramelised. Add the carrot, parsnip and celery and cook for about 15 minutes, or until tender.

Add the silverbeet to the pot, along with 4 litres of water and the thyme, parsley and bay leaf. Bring to the boil, reduce the heat to low, cover and simmer for about 1 hour, or until the stock is highly flavoured.

Remove the stock from the heat and strain through a fine sieve, pressing on the vegetables to extract all their juices. Pour into storage containers for the fridge or freezer. Discard the vegetables, unless you are keeping them to use in a soup. The stock can be refrigerated for 3–4 days or frozen for up to 3 months.

MAKES ABOUT 3.5 LITRES

I absolutely adore my new favourite noodles made from the humble zucchini. Who would have known that zucchini could taste so damn good? Recently I was asked to cook for one of the most prestigious resorts in the world, and I wanted to showcase nutritious recipes that would make people reconsider what they thought about food. After a morning class where I spoke about the problems associated with our modern dietary guidelines, I served a selection of mainly offal-based and above-ground green vegetable dishes. The response was amazing. I had children eating heart, liver and marrow. The breakthrough moment was when I served raw zucchini 'spaghetti' to a few Italians and they said they couldn't believe how fresh and delicious it was. Try this with a tomato sauce, a traditional bolognese or this simple pesto.

ZUCCHINI NOODLES WITH BASIL AND PARSLEY PESTO

1½ tablespoons coconut oil, ghee* or macadamia oil

3 zucchinis (about 500 g in total), cut into spaghetti strips on a mandoline or slicer

1 garlic clove, crushed

10 kalamata olives, pitted and halved

BASIL AND PARSLEY PESTO

2 large handfuls of basil leaves

2 large handfuls of flat-leaf parsley leaves

2 garlic cloves, coarsely chopped

1 tablespoon pine nuts, toasted

2 tablespoons lemon juice

12 macadamia nuts, toasted

125 ml (½ cup) macadamia oil or extra-virgin olive oil

sea salt and freshly ground black pepper

* See Glossary

To make the pesto, place all the ingredients in a mortar and pestle or food processor and combine to form a thick, coarse paste. Taste and adjust seasoning.

To make the noodles, heat the oil in a frying pan over medium–high heat. Add the zucchini and garlic and sauté for 1–1½ minutes, or until slightly soft. Season with salt and pepper, add the pesto and olives and toss well. Continue to cook for 1 minute, or until heated through. Spoon into bowls and serve.

SERVES 2

> TIP

You can also make noodles using a spiral spaghetti maker. It cuts a zucchini, carrot, beetroot or parsnip in one long, thin spiral. Kids love it!

Tomato and basil have got to be among the greatest flavour combinations of all time. Just ask the Italians, who use them in so many dishes, including caprese salad, spaghetti and meatballs and the most famous of all – the margherita pizza (named in honour of Queen Margherita in 1889 by a local Italian pizza maker). Here, I have replaced the buffalo mozzarella with cashew cheese to make it dairy free, but the rest is the same – tomato, basil and a crispy base to carry these amazing flavours.

MARGHERITA PIZZA

4 tablespoons Pizza Sauce (page 63)

2 tablespoons chopped flat-leaf parsley leaves

6 cherry tomatoes, sliced

100 g Cashew Cheese (page 218)

sea salt and freshly ground black pepper

8 basil leaves, to serve

2 macadamia nuts, grated, to serve

extra-virgin olive oil, to serve

PALEO PIZZA BASE

260 g (2½ cups) almond meal

130 g (1 cup) arrowroot* or tapioca flour*

1½ teaspoons baking powder

1 teaspoon sea salt

3 eggs

4 tablespoons macadamia oil or melted coconut oil

125 ml (½ cup) nut milk (to make your own, see page 258)

* See Glossary

To make the paleo pizza base, preheat the oven to 180°C. Line a large baking tray with baking paper.

Combine the almond meal, arrowroot or tapioca flour, baking powder and salt in a large bowl. In a separate bowl, whisk together the eggs, oil and nut milk.

Fold the egg mixture into the dry ingredients, one-third at a time, and mix thoroughly to form a smooth, thick dough.

Spoon the dough onto the prepared tray. Using a palette knife or spatula, spread the dough out in a round or rectangular shape to a thickness of 5 mm. You can make the pizza bases as big or small as you like depending on who it is for (kids usually love to have their own individual pizzas!). This amount of dough will make two 30 cm round pizza bases. Bake for 5 minutes until the pizza base is cooked through and lightly browned. Remove from the oven and set aside to cool.

Increase the oven to 240°C or as high as it will go.

Flip the pizza base and evenly spread over the pizza sauce. Scatter on the parsley and cherry tomato slices and dollop the cashew cheese on top. Season with salt and pepper. Return to the oven and cook for a further 5–10 minutes, or until golden and crisp.

Remove from the oven, cut into portions and garnish with the basil leaves, grated macadamias and a drizzle of olive oil.

SERVES 4

Kids adore sushi and I am stoked because it is usually their first introduction to raw fish and seaweed. When we have these at home we tend to put out an assortment of goodies and encourage the kids to try some new things. In this recipe the paleo crumbed prawns really set the bar high, but canned tuna, leftover roast chicken and soft-boiled eggs work a treat, too. Have fun with the combinations and you will be surprised at what the kids will come up with on their own.

NORI ROLLS WITH CRUMBED PRAWNS

150 g Cauliflower Rice (page 180)

1 tablespoon unhulled tahini

80 g (⅔ cup) tapioca flour*

3 eggs

155 g (1½ cups) almond meal

8 raw king prawns, shelled and deveined, with tails intact

sea salt

coconut oil, for deep-frying

freshly ground black pepper

4 toasted nori sheets

1 avocado, sliced

1 small Lebanese cucumber, julienned

½ carrot, julienned

5 cm piece of daikon (white radish), julienned

1 tablespoon black and white sesame seeds, toasted

tamari, to serve

pickled ginger, to serve (optional)

* See Glossary

Place the cauliflower rice and tahini in a bowl and mix until combined. Set aside.

Put the tapioca flour in a shallow bowl. Whisk the eggs and a dash of water in another shallow bowl. Place the almond meal in a third bowl.

Lightly season the prawns with salt, then dust with the tapioca flour, dip in the egg and roll in the almond meal, patting down firmly so each prawn is well covered.

Melt the oil in a saucepan over medium heat and when the oil reaches 160°C (a cube of bread dropped in the oil will turn golden brown in 30–35 seconds), fry the prawns for 1½–2 minutes until golden and crispy and cooked through.

Drain the the prawns on paper towel and season with salt and pepper.

Cut the nori sheets in half to form eight 10 cm × 18 cm sheets. Place a nori sheet, shiny side down, in the palm of your hand and top with some cauliflower rice, a prawn, some avocado, cucumber, carrot and daikon. Fold a bottom corner of the nori over the filling and then roll up to form a cone shape. Sprinkle over some sesame seeds. Repeat with the remaining ingredients. Serve immediately with the tamari as a dipping sauce and the pickled ginger, if using.

SERVES 4

I just had to include another cauliflower fried rice recipe in this book, even though one appears in *Healthy Every Day*. It really is a phenomenal dish that everyone loves. I cannot tell you how many positive emails and posts on social media I have had about this one simple little dish that replaces rice with cauliflower.

CAULIFLOWER FRIED RICE WITH PRAWNS

1 large cauliflower (about 800 g), separated into florets

2 tablespoons coconut oil

4 rashers of bacon or slices of ham, diced

200 g peeled and deveined raw prawns (about 400 g if you're buying them unpeeled)

4 eggs

2 splashes of fish sauce

1 onion, finely chopped

2 garlic cloves, finely chopped

½ red capsicum, diced

2.5 cm piece of ginger, finely grated

3 tablespoons tamari

sea salt or Himalayan salt

freshly ground white pepper

2 spring onions, thinly sliced

2 tablespoons chopped coriander leaves

2 tablespoons chopped flat-leaf parsley leaves

1 handful of bean sprouts, trimmed

finely chopped long red chilli, to serve (optional)

lime wedges, to serve

Pulse the cauliflower in a food processor until it resembles rice.

Melt a little coconut oil in a large wok or frying pan over high heat. Add the bacon or ham and fry until crispy. Remove and set aside. Wipe the pan clean, add a little more coconut oil and sauté the prawns over high heat for 2 minutes, or until lightly golden and almost cooked through. Remove from the pan and set aside.

Wipe the pan clean again, add a little more coconut oil and heat over medium–high heat. Whisk the eggs with a splash of fish sauce and pour into the pan. Tilt the pan to evenly distribute the eggs and cook for a couple of minutes to make a silky omelette. Remove, slice into thin strips and set aside.

Heat the remaining oil in the pan over high heat. Add the onion and garlic and cook for 3 minutes, or until softened. Stir in the capsicum and ginger and cook for 3–5 minutes. Add the cauliflower and cook for a few minutes until tender. Add the tamari, salt and pepper, spring onion, herbs, bean sprouts, bacon or ham, prawns and omelette strips and stir-fry for 1 minute until well combined and heated through.

Serve with a splash of fish sauce, some red chilli (if using) and lime wedges.

SERVES 4

Laksa is a dish that keeps you coming back for more as it is so fragrant and delicious. One of its key ingredients is turmeric, a spice that has been used for millennia for both culinary and medicinal purposes, and that packs a real nutritional punch. It has amazing anti-fungal, anti-inflammatory and antioxidant properties, and adds an earthy, warming flavour to dishes. I like to add fresh or powdered turmeric to a variety of recipes, from simple citrus juices to desserts such as coconut ice cream with manuka honey. But the most obvious use of turmeric is in aromatic curries, like this laksa. I have used kelp noodles instead of rice or egg noodles, however you can always omit them completely and just use more vegetables.

QUICK PRAWN LAKSA

250 g kelp noodles*

1 tablespoon coconut oil

3 × 400 ml cans coconut milk

2 tablespoons honey (optional)

½ teaspoon tamarind* paste

12 raw king prawns, peeled and deveined with tails intact

2½ tablespoons fish sauce

2½ tablespoons lime juice

¼ Chinese cabbage (wong bok), finely shredded

1 handful of bean sprouts

1 small handful of Thai basil leaves

1 small handful of coriander leaves

fried shallots (to make your own, see page 31)

2 limes, quartered

SPICE PASTE

6 garlic cloves, peeled

200 g long red chillies, roughly chopped

2 lemongrass stems, white part only, thinly sliced

1 teaspoon ground turmeric

5 kaffir lime leaves, finely shredded

* See Glossary

Soak the noodles in a bowl of cold water for 10 minutes to soften slightly.

Meanwhile, to make the spice paste, process the garlic, chilli, lemongrass, turmeric and lime leaves in a food processor or pound using a mortar and pestle until smooth.

Place the oil in a large saucepan over medium heat. Add the spice paste and fry for 2 minutes until fragrant. Add the coconut milk, honey (if using) and tamarind paste and bring to the boil. Add the prawns and bring back to the boil. Turn off the heat and allow to sit for 5 minutes until the prawns are just cooked through. Add the fish sauce, lime juice and cabbage. Return the pan to medium heat and cook for 1 minute.

Divide the noodles among four serving bowls and spoon on the laksa, making sure the prawns are divided evenly between the bowls. Garnish with the bean sprouts, basil, coriander and fried shallots. Serve with the lime quarters.

SERVES 4

Chorizo is a Spanish or Portuguese sausage made from pork, pork fat, salt and smoked paprika that has been fermented, cured and smoked. Try to find chorizo that uses organic, free-range pork. A lot of Spanish and Portuguese recipes team chorizo with seafood and it works a treat. Here I have married it with squid and a little romesco sauce to send your tastebuds to heaven!

BARBECUED SQUID WITH ROMESCO SAUCE

250 g truss cherry tomatoes

5 teaspoons coconut oil

½ teaspoon smoked paprika

salt and freshly ground black pepper

850 g baby squid tubes, cleaned, scored and cut into 3 cm × 5 cm pieces

3 smoked chorizo sausages, cut on an angle into 5 mm thick slices

1 lemon, cut into 5 mm thick slices

4 tablespoons extra-virgin olive oil

3 tablespoons red wine vinegar

2 handfuls of rocket leaves

1 handful of flat-leaf parsley leaves

80 g Ligurian or black olives, pitted

1 large fennel bulb, finely shaved

ROMESCO SAUCE

2 red capsicums, quartered

2 tomatoes, quartered

1 long red chilli, deseeded and chopped

1 teaspoon sweet paprika

1 tablespoon coconut oil, melted

salt and freshly ground black pepper

12 hazelnuts (activated if possible, see page 200), lightly toasted

12 blanched almonds, toasted

3 garlic cloves, chopped

2 tablespoons red wine vinegar

4 tablespoons extra-virgin olive oil

To make the romesco sauce, preheat the oven to 200°C. Place the capsicum, skin-side up, on a tray and bake for 10–15 minutes, or until the skin blackens. Place the capsicum in a bowl, cover with plastic wrap and set aside for 5 minutes. Peel off the skin, then chop the capsicum. Toss the tomato, chilli, paprika and coconut oil in a bowl and season with salt and pepper. Heat a chargrill pan over high heat, add the tomato and chilli and cook for 3–4 minutes until soft. Peel the tomato quarters and chop. Place the hazelnuts and almonds in a food processor and process until finely ground. Add the capsicum, tomato, chilli, garlic and vinegar and process to a paste. With the motor running, slowly add the olive oil and process until well combined. Season with salt and pepper, if necessary. Transfer to a bowl, cover with plastic wrap and refrigerate until needed.

Reduce the oven to 180°C. Soak four bamboo skewers in water to cover for 30 minutes. Line a baking tray with baking paper. Use scissors to cut the cherry tomatoes into 4 small bunches, leaving the truss intact. Place on the prepared tray and drizzle over 1 teaspoon of coconut oil. Season with the smoked paprika and salt and pepper. Bake for 8 minutes, or until the tomatoes soften slightly.

Meanwhile, lay a slice of chorizo inside each piece of squid and thread onto the skewers. Drizzle with the remaining coconut oil and season well.

Heat the barbecue or a chargrill pan to high. Add the skewers and lemon slices and cook for 2 minutes on the scored side and 1 minute on the other side, or until the squid is cooked and the lemon is caramelised.

Whisk the olive oil and red wine vinegar in a small bowl. Toss through the rocket, parsley, olives and fennel and season with salt and pepper.

To serve, smear romesco sauce on each plate and arrange the salad, lemon, tomatoes and skewers on top. Leftover romesco sauce can be stored in an airtight container in the fridge for up to 4 days.

SERVES 4

I can't think of a greater joy as a parent than when your kids start developing an appreciation for nature's superfoods. I never push my kids too hard to try things; instead we have an arrangement where if we are eating something new, they try a spoonful. If they don't like it, they don't have to eat it. However, they will be encouraged to try it again the next time we are eating it – which might be in a week's or 6 months' time. We do this because their palates are constantly changing and the more you experiment the more they will come to appreciate new flavours, aromas and textures. My heart skipped a beat recently when my eldest daughter, Chilli, tried a mussel for the twentieth time and said, 'Yum, Dad. Can I have another one?'.

MUSSELS WITH TOMATO AND BASIL

1 tablespoon ghee*

½ onion, chopped

4 garlic cloves, sliced

1 × 400 g can diced tomatoes

100 ml white wine

150 ml chicken stock (to make your own, see page 86)

1 kg mussels, scrubbed and debearded

1 handful of basil leaves, torn

sea salt and freshly ground black pepper

3 tablespoons lemon-infused olive oil

* See Glossary

Melt the ghee in a large saucepan over medium–high heat. Add the onion and garlic and sauté for 2–4 minutes, or until soft. Stir in the tomatoes, wine and stock, mix well and bring to the boil. Add the mussels, cover and cook for 3–4 minutes, or until the mussels open. Holding down the lid, shake the pan to redistribute the mussels. Discard any mussels that do not open.

Add the basil to the mussels and mix well. Season with salt and black pepper. Divide the mussels between two large bowls; pour over the broth, drizzle with the lemon-infused olive oil and serve immediately.

SERVES 2

> **VARIATION**

If you like a bit of spice, thinly slice 1 long red chilli and add it to the pan with the onion and garlic.

If you are entertaining and really want to show off in the kitchen, look no further than this sashimi dish. Seriously, to slice some spanking fresh raw fish and arrange it on a platter with a simple dipping sauce almost feels like cheating because it is so simple. The key is to get your hands on the best possible wild and sustainable fish that you love to eat raw – think tuna, kingfish, scallops, prawns, squid, flathead, snapper and, of course, sea urchins and oysters (you don't have to slice these last two beauties) – and slice nice and evenly. Don't worry if the slices are a bit thick, they don't need to be paper thin. I like to serve sashimi with some daikon and seaweed for their amazing nutritional properties.

SASHIMI WITH JAPANESE DRESSING

240 g sashimi-grade fish (such as tuna, ocean trout, Atlantic salmon, kingfish, scallops or prawns)

wasabi, to taste

pickled ginger (optional)

JAPANESE DRESSING

100 ml tamari

1 teaspoon finely grated ginger

2 tablespoons dried bonito flakes*

½ teaspoon sesame oil

* See Glossary

To make the dressing, combine all the dressing ingredients in a bowl and allow to stand for at least 1 hour or, for best results, overnight. Strain.

Thinly slice your fish with a very sharp knife and arrange on a platter with the wasabi and pickled ginger, if using. Serve with the dressing.

SERVES 2

Walk into any restaurant/cafe/pub these days and you will notice they have 'sliders' on their menu. A slider is basically a small burger that is taking the world by storm. If we could just ditch the bun, the cheese and the fries that are usually cooked in trans fats, then we are on our way to optimal health. We love making burgers at home and they come in lots of different forms, depending on the protein – beef, pork, lamb, chook, fish, prawns or crabmeat – and what we choose to season them with. This recipe uses fish but feel free to use your favourite meat – you can't go wrong.

SALMON SLIDERS

400 g salmon fillets, skinned, pin-boned and finely chopped or minced in a food processor

3 tablespoons chopped flat-leaf parsley leaves

1 garlic clove, finely chopped

1 French shallot, finely chopped

1 spring onion, green part thinly sliced and white part finely chopped

1 egg

juice of 1 lemon

Himalayan salt and freshly ground black pepper

2 tablespoons coconut oil, melted

16 field mushrooms (about 6–7 cm in diameter), stems removed

½ Lebanese cucumber, thinly sliced

2 tomatoes, thinly sliced

½ red onion, thinly sliced

3 iceberg lettuce leaves, shredded

mayonnaise (to make your own, see page 58), to serve

sesame seeds, to serve

In a large bowl, combine the salmon, parsley, garlic, shallot, spring onion, egg and lemon juice and mix until well combined. Season with salt and pepper. Roll into six balls, then carefully press down to flatten into patties around 6 cm in diameter – you should get about 8 patties. (The mixture will be a little wet so take care when rolling.)

Heat 1 tablespoon of the coconut oil in a large frying pan over medium heat and fry the patties, in batches, for 2–4 minutes on each side until golden and cooked through. Drain on paper towel and season with salt and pepper.

Preheat the oven to 180°C. Line a baking tray with baking paper.

Place the mushrooms stem-side down on the prepared tray. Drizzle with the remaining tablespoon of coconut oil, season with salt and pepper and roast in the oven for 10 minutes, or until tender. Place the mushrooms on paper towel to remove the excess moisture. Allow to cool.

To assemble, lay eight cooked mushrooms, flat side up, on a workbench or platter. Top each with a salmon patty, some cucumber, tomato, red onion and lettuce and a dollop of mayonnaise. Place the eight remaining cooked mushrooms on top, flat side down, and sprinkle with the sesame seeds. Insert a small skewer directly in the centre of the slider to hold the filling in place and serve.

SERVES 4

Seafood is nature's ultimate fast food. It takes less time to create many wonderful seafood dishes than it does to pick up the phone and order takeaway. I used wild kingfish in the photo as my mate had caught one the day before and gave me some. Cheers, Udo. You can use any fish you like, as long as it is wild and sustainable. The salsa verde is a paleo version: I omit the bread, which doesn't affect the flavour at all, and team it with a wonderfully simple and fresh salad.

ROASTED KINGFISH WITH SALSA VERDE

1 side kingfish belly, skin on (800 g–1 kg)

1–2 tablespoons coconut oil, melted

1 handful of flat-leaf parsley leaves

1 handful of mint leaves

1 small handful of dill

1 handful of mâche* leaves

3 radishes, thinly sliced

1 small fennel bulb, shaved

4 tablespoons extra-virgin olive oil

2 tablespoons apple cider vinegar

sea salt and freshly ground black pepper

lemon wedges, to serve

SALSA VERDE

½ green capsicum, finely diced

1 French shallot, finely diced

2 garlic cloves, crushed

3 tablespoons capers, chopped

3 tablespoons finely diced gherkins

2 anchovy fillets, finely chopped

1 handful of flat-leaf parsley leaves, finely chopped

1 small handful of mint leaves, finely chopped

1 tablespoon finely chopped preserved lemon

2 tablespoons pine nuts, toasted

1 small handful of basil leaves, finely chopped

2 tablespoons finely chopped tarragon leaves

grated zest and juice of 1 lemon

125 ml (½ cup) extra-virgin olive oil

salt and freshly ground black pepper

* See Glossary

To make the salsa verde, combine all the ingredients in a bowl and mix well. Add a little more lemon juice if you prefer the salsa verde to have a sharper flavour and add more olive oil if needed. Set aside.

Preheat the oven to 240°C. Place a baking tray in the oven for 10 minutes to get really hot.

Score the kingfish skin with a sharp knife, making a few incisions diagonally across the fish. Rub over some coconut oil and season with salt and pepper.

Carefully remove the tray from the oven and lightly grease it with a little coconut oil. Place the kingfish on the tray, skin-side down, and return the tray to the oven. Cook for 5 minutes. Turn the oven to the grill setting. Place the tray directly beneath the grill and cook for about 1–2 minutes, or until the flesh is lightly caramelised and just cooked through.

Place the parsley, mint, dill, mâche leaves, radishes and fennel in a bowl and gently toss.

Whisk the olive oil and vinegar in a small bowl and season with salt and pepper to make a simple dressing. Drizzle a little dressing over the salad and gently toss, adding more if needed.

Place the fish on a platter and spoon over the salsa verde. Serve with the lemon wedges and the salad.

SERVES 4

This meal is such a winner. I usually serve snapper as a whole fish, but I wanted to make this as accessible as possible, so I have used fillets. Once you have everyone in the family converted to this dish, then you can prepare whole fish the same way. The reason I love using whole fish is that they are usually fresher, cheaper and more nutritious because you get to eat all of it. Whatever is leftover can be turned into a delicious fish stock for a soup or curry. Play around with the veggies in this dish – Asian mushrooms are delicious, as are asparagus, okra and zucchini.

STEAMED SNAPPER WITH GINGER, TAMARI AND SESAME

4 snapper fillets (about 180 g each), bones removed

5 cm piece of ginger, julienned

1–2 long red chillies, deseeded and finely sliced (optional)

2 spring onions, thinly sliced, plus extra to serve

2 teaspoons fish sauce

375 ml (1½ cups) fish or chicken stock (to make your own, see pages 86–87)

3 tablespoons tamari

1 garlic clove, finely chopped

¼ Chinese cabbage (wong bok), trimmed and leaves separated and sliced

2 teaspoons sesame oil

1 tablespoon coconut oil

black and white sesame seeds, toasted, to serve

Cauliflower Rice (page 180), to serve

Line a large steamer basket with baking paper. Place the snapper in a single layer on top. Scatter over the ginger, chilli (if using) and spring onion and drizzle on some fish sauce. Cover and steam over a wok or saucepan of simmering water for 4–6 minutes, or until the fish is cooked through.

Meanwhile, place the stock in a saucepan over medium heat. Add the tamari and garlic and bring to the boil. Add the cabbage, cover and cook for 3–4 minutes, or until the cabbage is tender. Give the cabbage a toss halfway through to make sure it cooks evenly. Season with salt and pepper and keep warm.

Heat the sesame oil and coconut oil in a small saucepan for 1–2 minutes until smoking.

Transfer the fish to serving plates. Ladle over some tamari broth and Chinese cabbage, then pour on the hot oil. Scatter over the extra spring onion, sprinkle over some sesame seeds and serve with the cauliflower rice. Season with a touch more fish sauce or salt if needed.

SERVES 4

Whiting is a delicious fish and it is a good one to introduce to kids at a young age – just make sure there are no bones. I have been catching whiting for years at Bondi Beach and I never tire of watching the end of my rod twitch as the whiting investigate the worm at the end of the hook. To catch and cook your own breakfast, lunch or dinner is one of life's true joys. Here I serve the whiting with a divine tomato dressing (sauce vierge). It takes only minutes to prepare, and is the perfect accompaniment for any seafood, whether it is white fish, grilled scallops, oysters or barbecued prawns.

CRISPY-SKINNED WHITING WITH TOMATO DRESSING

3 bunches of asparagus, trimmed

2 garlic cloves, chopped

3 tablespoons coconut oil or other good-quality fat*, melted

sea salt and freshly ground black pepper

4 × 160 g whiting fillets

finely grated zest of 1 lemon (optional)

TOMATO DRESSING

125 ml (½ cup) olive oil

1 tablespoon coriander seeds, toasted and crushed

200 g cherry tomatoes, quartered

4 tablespoons lemon juice

1 large handful of basil leaves, torn

* See Glossary

Preheat the oven to 200°C.

Place the asparagus on a baking tray in a single layer. Sprinkle on the garlic, drizzle on 2 tablespoons of the oil or fat and season with salt and pepper. Roast for 8–10 minutes, or until tender.

Meanwhile, for the tomato dressing, gently heat the oil to about 80°C in a saucepan over low heat. Add the crushed coriander seeds, tomato, lemon juice and basil and heat for 1 minute, or until warmed through. Keep warm.

Preheat a barbecue or chargrill pan to high. Rub the whiting fillets with the remaining tablespoon of oil or fat, season with salt and pepper and cook for 1–2 minutes on each side until rare to medium–rare.

Arrange the asparagus on four serving plates. Top with a piece of fish, spoon on the tomato dressing, add a sprinkle of lemon zest, if desired, and grind on some pepper.

SERVES 4

When it comes to seafood, many people feel unsure of how best to cook it. My advice is firstly to cultivate a relationship with a fishmonger or the fish seller at your local farmers market and search out local, wild-caught varieties that are seasonal and therefore cheaper. Secondly, build up a repertoire of simple seafood recipes like this one, which works well with pretty much any seafood, including white flesh fish, prawns, scallops, squid, bugs, mussels or clams. This stir-fry has become one of my family's favourites and it is perfect for when you need to whip up some dinner in a hurry.

FISH STIR-FRY WITH GINGER AND CHILLI

2 tablespoons coconut oil or other good-quality fat*

5 cm piece of ginger, peeled and julienned

2 long red chillies (or more if you like it hot), sliced

2 spring onions, white and green parts, cut into 5 cm batons

4 garlic cloves, thinly sliced

750 g white flesh fish fillets (try to source fish that is local to your area), skinned and cut into 4 cm pieces

300 g Chinese broccoli (gai larn), trimmed and roughly chopped

1 large handful of coriander leaves, to serve

sesame seeds, toasted, to serve

SAUCE

100 ml tamari

1½ tablespoons fish sauce

1½ teaspoons sesame oil

1 teaspoon freshly ground black pepper

2 tablespoons chicken or fish stock (to make your own, see pages 86–87)

2 teaspoons honey (optional)

* See Glossary

Mix the sauce ingredients in a small bowl with 120 ml of water and set aside.

Heat the oil or fat in a wok or large frying pan over medium heat. When hot, add the ginger, chilli, spring onion and garlic and stir-fry for 1 minute, or until fragrant. Add the fish and stir-fry for 2–3 minutes until the fish is half cooked. Pour in the sauce, add the Chinese broccoli and continue to stir-fry for a further 2–3 minutes until the fish is cooked through and the Chinese broccoli is tender.

Serve in individual bowls or on a large platter, garnished with the coriander and sesame seeds.

SERVES 4–6

I absolutely love this recipe and I am sure you and your family will, too. It is perfect for a kid's birthday party. You can also use prawns, scallops, chicken or pork fillets. I have teamed the filling here with lettuce cup 'tacos', as I love the freshness of the lettuce and the fun way you can hold it all in there. However, if you want to go the more traditional route, then I have a paleo tortilla recipe on page 141 that fits the bill perfectly. Then, if you like, just add some guacamole and coleslaw.

FISH TACOS WITH CELERIAC REMOULADE

500 g flathead fillets (or any firm white fish), skinned and pin-boned

60 g (½ cup) tapioca flour*

2 eggs, lightly beaten with 3 tablespoons water

100 g (1 cup) almond meal or 60 g (1 cup) desiccated coconut

coconut oil or ghee* for deep-frying

8 butter lettuce leaves

Guacamole (page 197), to serve

lemon halves, to serve

CELERIAC REMOULADE

240 g celeriac, peeled

2 red radishes, julienned

125 g (½ cup) aioli (to make your own, see page 172)

1 tablespoon finely chopped chervil leaves

1 tablespoon finely chopped flat-leaf parsley leaves

juice and zest of 1 lemon

Himalayan salt or sea salt and freshly ground black pepper

* See Glossary

To make the celeriac remoulade, grate the celeriac or julienne it using a mandoline. Celeriac tends to discolour quickly, so place it in cold water. Combine the radish, aioli, chervil, parsley and lemon juice in a bowl and season to taste. Drain the celeriac, pat dry on paper towel and stir it into the aioli mixture. Taste for seasoning and transfer to a small bowl.

Cut the flathead into eight even portions.

Place the tapioca flour in a shallow bowl, the egg mixture in another shallow bowl and the almond meal or coconut in a third bowl.

Season the fish with some salt, dust lightly with the tapioca flour, dip in the egg mixture and coat with the almond meal or coconut, pressing them on firmly.

Heat the coconut oil or ghee to 160°C in a wok or large saucepan. (To test the temperature, drop a small piece of fish in the oil – it should bubble instantly around the edges.) Working in batches, fry the fish for 90 seconds until cooked through. Drain on paper towel and season with salt.

Place the lettuce leaves, remoulade, guacamole, fish and lemon wedges on a serving platter and let everyone help themselves. To assemble your lettuce cup 'tacos', fill each lettuce leaf with some remoulade, guacamole and a piece of fish and squeeze the lemon juice over the top.

SERVES 4

There are healing properties in a bowl of chicken soup that people have known about for centuries. Chicken and other bone broths are especially soothing if you have any sort of digestive problem. These broths contain numerous minerals that are easily assimilated by the body: calcium, magnesium, phosphorous, silicon and many other trace minerals and amino acids. They also provide chondroitin sulphates and glucosamine that help with arthritis and joint pain. And we cannot forget about gelatine, the ingredient in broths that strengthens the gut wall, reduces inflammation and helps with so many illnesses. It is essential to make the stock yourself for this soup.

CHICKEN NOODLE SOUP

2 tablespoons coconut oil or other good-quality fat*

1 onion, chopped

3 garlic cloves, crushed

2 carrots, chopped

2 celery stalks, halved lengthways, and cut into 1 cm chunks

4 thyme sprigs

1 bay leaf

1.25 litres chicken stock (page 86)

150 g kelp noodles*, roughly chopped

300 g (1½ cups) finely shredded leftover cooked chicken

sea salt and freshly ground black pepper

1 handful of flat-leaf parsley leaves, finely chopped

* See Glossary

Heat the oil or fat in a stockpot or large saucepan over medium heat. Add the onion, garlic, carrot, celery, thyme and bay leaf. Cook, stirring regularly, for about 6 minutes until the vegetables are softened but not browned. Pour in the chicken stock and bring to the boil. Reduce the heat to low and simmer for 20 minutes.

Add the noodles to the pan and simmer for 5 minutes until tender. Stir in the chicken and simmer for a few minutes to heat through. Season with salt and pepper and sprinkle with the parsley before serving.

SERVES 4

▶ **VARIATION**

You can substitute cauliflower rice (page 180), zucchini noodles (page 88) or parsnip noodles (page 154) for the kelp noodles if you like.

Young coconuts are bloody awesome, from the sweet, energising water contained inside to the jelly-like flesh that you are left with. They can be a bit tricky to open (see page 285 for instructions). Young coconut flesh can be used in many different ways – you can blend it into a salad dressing to give a lovely, creamy consistency; finely chop it and add it to desserts; pop it into smoothies to thicken them; or use it in salads such as this one. I have served this salad in 'bowls' made from half a young coconut, but don't worry – if you damage the delicate flesh then just shred it and put it through the salad and serve it in the coconut husk or your favourite bowl instead. And if you like it hot, feel free to add as much red chilli to the dressing as you like.

YOUNG-COCONUT CHICKEN SALAD

2 young coconuts*

500 g chicken thigh fillets

2 × 400 ml cans coconut milk

2 tablespoons fish sauce

1 large garlic clove, crushed

1 tablespoon peeled and grated ginger

300 g (4 cups) finely shredded cabbage

2 large handfuls of coriander leaves

1 handful of mint leaves

1 handful of Thai basil leaves

1 small carrot, shredded or grated

3 tablespoons fried shallots (to make your own, see page 31)

2 tablespoons fried garlic (to make your own, see page 31)

80 g (½ cup) almonds (activated if possible, see page 200), crushed

PICKLED ONION

½ red onion, thinly sliced

3 tablespoons apple cider vinegar

FISH SAUCE DRESSING

100 ml fish sauce

2 tablespoons grated ginger

3 garlic cloves, crushed

1 small red chilli, finely chopped

juice of 3 limes, or more to taste

1 tablespoon honey (optional)

* See Glossary

To make the pickled onion, combine the onion and vinegar in a bowl and let sit for 20 minutes. Drain.

To prepare the coconut bowls, use a large, sharp, heavy knife to cut the coconuts in half. Pour out the coconut water and reserve for another use. Gently ease a large spoon between the flesh and skin and, in a circular motion and trying not to break the flesh, run the spoon around the side of the coconut. Carefully slide the spoon underneath to the base and lift out the coconut flesh. Repeat with the remaining coconut halves.

Place the chicken thighs in a saucepan and add the coconut milk, 250 ml of water, the fish sauce, garlic and ginger and bring to the boil. Reduce the heat and simmer for 10–12 minutes, or until the chicken is cooked through. Set aside to cool. When the chicken is cool enough to handle, shred the meat.

To make the fish sauce dressing, combine all the ingredients plus 100 ml of water in a bowl or large jar. Taste and add more lime juice or water, if necessary.

Combine the cabbage, coriander, mint, basil and carrot in a large bowl and toss well.

When you're ready to serve, toss the chicken into the salad and add the dressing to taste. Place the salad in the coconut bowls and top with the fried shallots, fried garlic, crushed almonds and pickled onion.

SERVES 4

One of my goals in life is to write a roast chicken bible. I have cooked Moroccan, Indonesian, Chinese, Korean, Japanese, Indian, Ethiopian, English, Italian, French, Spanish, Portuguese, South American, Jamaican, Mexican, Fijian, Vietnamese, Thai and Burmese roast chickens, to name just a few! It is a great way to get kids to expand their palates, as you are giving them something that is very familiar, but adding different spices and herbs. This recipe is a flavour-filled version of an Italian-inspired chicken dish my friend Marina has cooked for me a number of times. I especially like it when the lemon gets a bit burnt in the tray and the juices mix with the chicken fat, garlic and thyme to form the most delicious sauce. Belissimo!

ROAST CHICKEN WITH GARLIC AND THYME

2 garlic bulbs, cloves separated and unpeeled

1 bunch of thyme

1 parsnip, thickly sliced lengthways

1 onion, unpeeled, thickly sliced

1 carrot, thickly sliced lengthways

1 × 1.8 kg chicken

3 tablespoons coconut oil or other good-quality fat*, melted

sea salt and freshly ground black pepper

1 lemon, halved

450 ml chicken stock (to make your own, see page 86)

3 tablespoons dry white wine

Roasted Vegetables (page 188) or Sweet Potato Smash (page 182), to serve

Simple Garden Salad (page 168), to serve

* See Glossary

Preheat the oven to 200°C.

Scatter two-thirds of the garlic and half the thyme in the base of a large roasting tin. Arrange the parsnip, onion and carrot in the tin.

Rinse the chicken inside and out, pat dry with paper towel, rub with the oil or fat and season generously inside and out with salt and pepper. Stuff half the lemon into the cavity along with the remaining garlic and thyme. Place the chicken in the roasting tin, squeeze on the juice of the remaining lemon and pour in 125 ml of the stock. Roast, basting occasionally with the pan juices, for 30 minutes. Reduce the heat to 170°C and cook for a further 30–45 minutes, or until golden and the juices run clear when the thigh is pierced with a skewer.

Remove the chicken from the tin, cover with foil and rest in a warm place for 10 minutes.

To make a beautiful gravy, discard the skins from the onion and garlic and place the roasting tin over medium heat on the stovetop. Pour in the remaining stock and the white wine and bring to the boil. Using a flat wooden spoon, stir the base to dislodge any cooked-in bits. Once the pan juices have come to the boil, remove the tin from the heat. Transfer the vegetables and pan juices to a blender and blend until smooth. (Take care when blending the hot liquid.) Add more stock or water, if the gravy is too thick. Season with salt and pepper. If you prefer a nice smooth gravy and you find yours has little bits in it, pass it through a fine sieve into a serving bowl or jug.

Carve the chicken and serve with the roasted vegetables or sweet potato mash and a garden salad.

SERVES 4–6

The classic schnitzel is a fillet of meat, most often veal as in the Vienna schnitzel from Austria, which is thinly sliced and tenderised, then dusted lightly in seasoned flour, dipped in egg and dredged in breadcrumbs before being pan-fried in oil or butter until golden and crispy. This paleo version is equally tasty but a lot better for you! I use arrowroot or coconut flour instead of wheat flour to dust, and the crumbing mix is almond meal mixed with some spices. For extra crunch, you can also add finely chopped nuts or seeds, or even shredded coconut, to your crumbing mix.

CHICKEN SCHNITZEL WITH SLAW

4 chicken breast fillets

200 g (2 cups) almond meal, plus extra if needed

2 teaspoons garlic powder

2 teaspoons onion powder

1 teaspoon chilli powder

2 teaspoons dried parsley

sea salt and freshly ground black pepper

60 g (½ cup) arrowroot*

3 eggs

4 tablespoons coconut milk

400 ml coconut oil

Coleslaw with Chervil Dressing (page 172), to serve

lemon wedges, to serve

* See Glossary

Place the chicken between two sheets of baking paper and pound with a meat mallet until about 1 cm thick.

Combine the almond meal and dried spices in a shallow bowl and mix well. Season with salt and pepper and set aside.

Place the tapioca flour in another shallow bowl.

In a third bowl, whisk the eggs and coconut milk until well combined.

Dust the pounded chicken with the tapioca flour, shaking off any excess. Working with one piece at a time, dip the chicken in the egg mixture, then evenly coat with the almond meal mixture.

Heat the coconut oil in a large, deep frying pan over medium–high heat until it reaches about 160°C. (To test, place a tiny piece of chicken into the oil – if it starts to bubble around the chicken immediately, the oil is ready.) Shallow fry the crumbed chicken for 3–5 minutes on both sides, or until golden and cooked through. Remove from the pan and place on paper towel to soak up the excess oil. Season with some salt and pepper.

Serve the chicken schnitzels with the coleslaw and lemon wedges.

SERVES 4

Anything on a stick seems to win everyone over at dinnertime. This is another great recipe to get the kids involved. I always have disposable gloves in the kitchen for messy jobs, which makes it a lot easier cleaning up, and if using turmeric or beetroot, then our hands and fingers aren't stained. I serve these skewers with a raw and utterly delicious peanut-free satay sauce, which you can whip up in a matter of minutes.

SATAY CHICKEN SKEWERS

800 g chicken thigh fillets, cut into 2.5 cm cubes

sea salt and freshly ground black pepper

coriander leaves, to serve

lime wedges, to serve

MARINADE

1½ teaspoons lime zest

1½ tablespoons lime juice

1 tablespoon coconut oil, melted, plus extra for cooking

3 tablespoons tamari

3 tablespoons fish sauce

3 garlic cloves, crushed

1½ tablespoons finely grated ginger

1½ tablespoons ground turmeric

1½ teaspoons ground coriander

1 teaspoon ground cumin

2 teaspoons sea salt

CASHEW SATAY SAUCE

160 g (1 cup) cashews (activated if possible, see page 200)

120 g (½ cup) almond butter

2 tablespoons finely grated ginger

1 long red chilli, deseeded and finely chopped

2 tablespoons tamari

1 tablespoon sesame oil

1 tablespoon maple syrup

sea salt

To make the marinade, combine all the ingredients in a large bowl and mix well. Add the chicken and toss until thoroughly coated. Cover and marinate for at least 2 hours, or refrigerate overnight.

Soak 8 bamboo skewers in a shallow dish of cold water for at least 30 minutes. Drain.

To make the cashew satay sauce, combine the cashews and almond butter in a food processor and pulse until the nuts are well ground. Add the ginger and chilli and process until well blended. Add the tamari, sesame oil and maple syrup and blend well. Gradually pour in 4 tablespoons of water and pulse until the sauce becomes smooth. If the sauce is a little too thick, simply add more water. Transfer to a serving bowl and set aside. Season with a little salt if desired.

Preheat a barbecue or chargrill plate to medium–high.

Thread the marinated chicken cubes onto the prepared skewers and season with salt and pepper. Grill the skewers, basting with the marinade and turning often, for 6–8 minutes until browned and cooked through.

Warm the satay dipping sauce, if desired. Scatter the coriander leaves over the skewers and serve with lime wedges and the satay sauce on the side.

SERVES 4

We are always looking for ways to 'jazz up' (as my beautiful mum would say) our food. I can think of no better place to start than with the spice drawer. Spices can turn a simple piece of chicken, meat or seafood into a culinary delight. This recipe takes its inspiration from Jamaica, with the use of jerk seasoning. Let the flavours make your kitchen the most intoxicating and seductive place to be. You will need to start this recipe a day ahead.

JAMAICAN JERK CHICKEN

1 kg chicken drumsticks

2 bay leaves

2 tablespoons coconut oil

lime wedges, to serve

1 handful of coriander leaves, to serve

Roasted Vegetables (page 188), to serve

JERK MARINADE

1 red onion, chopped

3 spring onions, chopped

6 large garlic cloves, crushed

4 scotch bonnets* or habanero chillies*, deseeded and chopped

3 tablespoons lime juice

3 tablespoons tamari or coconut aminos*

3 tablespoons coconut oil, melted

1 tablespoon white wine vinegar

1 tablespoon honey (optional)

1 tablespoon thyme leaves

1 tablespoon paprika

2 teaspoons ground allspice

2 teaspoons freshly ground black pepper

1½ teaspoons sea salt

½ teaspoon ground cinnamon

¼ teaspoon freshly grated nutmeg

* See Glossary

To make the jerk marinade, combine all the ingredients in a food processor and process to a smooth paste.

Transfer the marinade to a large shallow bowl, add the chicken and bay leaves and turn the chicken to coat. Cover and refrigerate overnight for best results.

Preheat the oven to 200°C.

Bring the chicken to room temperature 20 minutes before cooking.

Heat the oil in a large frying pan over medium–high heat. Add the chicken drumsticks, in batches, and seal, basting occasionally with the marinade, for 5 minutes, or until browned on all sides. Place the chicken in a roasting tin and roast in the oven for 20–25 minutes, or until the chicken is cooked all the way through. Cover with foil and allow to rest for 5 minutes before serving

Arrange the chicken and lime wedges on a platter and sprinkle over the coriander leaves. Serve with roasted vegetables.

SERVES 4

When I opened my first restaurant more than 20 years ago, we made a grilled chicken Caesar salad and we sold more of these than any other item on the lunch menu. The great thing about salads is that you don't need a huge amount of protein – 60–90 grams per person is more than satisfying when you also include heaps of fresh salad leaves, vegetables, nuts, seeds and an amazing dressing. I always cook up more chicken than I need when doing a roast chook, so that I have some left over to use in salads like this.

CHICKEN SALAD WITH AVOCADO RANCH DRESSING

2 chicken breast fillets, skin left on

2 tablespoons coconut oil or other good-quality fat*, melted

4 celery hearts with leaves, chopped

2 granny smith apples, cored and thinly sliced

2 witlof, leaves separated and torn

1 large handful of curly endive leaves

1 large handful of mâche* leaves

½ bunch of tarragon leaves, torn

40 g (⅓ cup) raisins

35 g (⅓ cup) walnuts (activated if possible, see page 200), chopped

80 ml (⅓ cup) extra-virgin olive oil

2 tablespoons apple cider vinegar

AVOCADO RANCH DRESSING

1 avocado, mashed

2 tablespoons extra-virgin olive oil or macadamia nut oil

2 tablespoons coconut cream

1 tablespoon apple cider vinegar

1 tablespoon chopped flat-leaf parsley leaves

1 tablespoon chopped dill

1 teaspoon Dijon mustard or Fermented Mustard (page 177)

½ teaspoon onion powder

salt and freshly ground black pepper

* See Glossary

To make the ranch dressing, combine the avocado, 4 tablespoons of water, the oil, coconut cream, vinegar, parsley, dill, mustard and onion powder in a food processor and process until smooth. Season to taste with salt and pepper.

Transfer the dressing to a bowl, cover with plastic wrap and refrigerate until needed.

Preheat the oven to 200°C.

Rub the chicken breasts with some of the oil or fat and season with salt and pepper. Heat the remaining oil in a large frying pan over medium–high heat and sear the chicken, skin-side down, until crisp and lightly golden (about 2 minutes). Turn the chicken over and sear on the other side for about 1 minute, or until lightly golden. Transfer the chicken to a baking tray and roast, skin-side up, for 7 minutes until cooked through. Remove from the oven and allow to cool.

Separate the crispy skin from the chicken and slice the skin into small strips. Cut the flesh into 1 cm thick slices and set aside.

To make the salad, combine the celery, apple, witlof, curly endive, mâche, tarragon, raisins and walnuts in a bowl. Mix together the olive oil and vinegar and drizzle over the salad. Add the chicken slices and crispy skin strips and season with salt and pepper. Toss to combine.

To serve, transfer the salad to a serving platter or bowl and drizzle over some of the ranch dressing. Pass the remaining dressing at the table.

SERVES 4

The paleo way of life is not meant to be restrictive, as you can see from this lovely butter chicken recipe. All the nasties have been replaced with good-quality ingredients that make it as good, if not better, than the original. I prefer chicken thighs for their superior flavour and tenderness. And be adventurous with your vegetable component. Try eggplant, okra, zucchini, asparagus, pumpkin, sweet potato and Asian water spinach. The rice has been replaced with cauliflower 'rice' but broccoli 'rice' is also a big hit or try a mixture of both.

BUTTER CHICKEN

120 g ghee*

1 large onion, diced

4 garlic cloves, crushed

2 teaspoons garam masala

1 teaspoon ground cardamom

1 teaspoon ground coriander

1 teaspoon ground ginger

1 teaspoon ground cumin

½ teaspoon paprika

1–2 pinches of cayenne pepper (optional)

1 teaspoon ground turmeric

3 tablespoons tomato paste

1 teaspoon sea salt

2 tablespoons lemon juice

1 × 400 ml can coconut cream

700 g chicken thigh fillets, cut into bite-sized pieces

coriander leaves, to serve

Cauliflower Rice (page 180), to serve

* See Glossary

Heat 4 tablespoons of the ghee in a large saucepan over medium heat. Add the onion and sauté for 3 minutes until translucent. Turn the heat down to low and stir in the garlic and spices. Add the tomato paste and cook for 1 minute. Add the salt, lemon juice, coconut cream and the remainder of the ghee and mix well.

Turn the heat up to medium and bring the sauce to a simmer. Add the chicken and stir until well coated with the sauce. Cover the pan with a lid and cook, stirring occasionally, for 20–25 minutes, or until the chicken is cooked through and the sauce has thickened.

Garnish with the coriander and serve with the cauliflower rice.

SERVES 4

Rosemary, garlic and lemon. Whenever I think about these three ingredients, all I see is roast chicken in all its glory. The purpose of this book is to offer real-life solutions to time-poor families who value their health, and this recipe fits the bill perfectly. It takes very little time and uses just a few quality ingredients that most families will have on hand. I have chosen marylands here as they are quicker to cook than a whole bird. For an even quicker meal, use wings. Serve with a big bowl of roasted veggies or a salad.

ROAST CHICKEN WITH ROSEMARY, GARLIC AND LEMON

80 g coconut oil or other good-quality fat*, melted

2 tablespoons honey (optional)

1 teaspoon paprika

1 teaspoon onion powder

1 tablespoon Italian seasoning

¼ teaspoon dried chilli flakes

sea salt and freshly ground black pepper

4 chicken marylands (about 1.2 kg in total)

2 lemons, quartered

1 garlic bulb, halved across the cloves

4 French shallots, peeled and halved

1 teaspoon dried oregano

3 rosemary sprigs, torn into pieces

chopped herbs (such as rosemary, thyme, flat-leaf parsley), to serve

* See Glossary

In a small bowl, whisk together the oil or fat, honey (if using), paprika, onion powder, Italian seasoning, chilli flakes and salt and pepper.

Place the chicken in a roasting tin and spread out the pieces so they cook evenly. Pour the oil mixture over the chicken, turning to coat on all sides. Arrange the lemon, garlic and shallot around and under the chicken and sprinkle on the herbs. For best results, cover the chicken and place in the fridge to marinate for at least 2 hours or overnight.

Preheat the oven to 190°C.

Season the chicken with salt and pepper and roast for 25–30 minutes, or until the chicken is cooked through, the skin is crispy and the juices run clear when pierced with the tip of a knife. (Remove the garlic if it's starting to darken too quickly and return to the pan 2 minutes before the chicken is ready.) Garnish with the chopped herbs and serve with roasted vegetables. Squeeze over the roasted lemon wedges at the table.

SERVES 4

I learnt this recipe from San Francisco chef Leo Beckerman, who has the coolest little Jewish deli called Wise Sons in the Mission District. This is his grandmother's recipe and he makes it the old-fashioned way by using chicken fat (schmaltz). Chicken fat is hard to come by these days, so you can use any quality animal fat such as duck fat, lard, tallow or ghee, or coconut oil would work well too. The key is to use organic, free-range chicken or duck livers, which means the birds have not been given antibiotics or hormones. You can substitute beef, lamb, pork, or kangaroo liver for the chicken or duck with excellent results. I like to eat this with some fermented veggies and seed crackers or paleo bread.

WISE SONS' CHOPPED LIVER

550 g chicken livers

sea salt and freshly ground black pepper

2 tablespoons coconut oil or other good-quality fat*, melted

1 large onion, finely chopped

1 garlic clove, crushed

pinch of paprika

1 bay leaf

1 thyme sprig, leaves picked and chopped

1 flat-leaf parsley sprig, leaves picked and chopped

1½ tablespoons brandy (optional)

1½ tablespoons chicken stock (to make your own, see page 86)

2 hard-boiled eggs, grated (optional)

Seed Crackers (page 204) or Seed and Nut Bread (page 23), to serve

Cultured Carrots (page 171) or Beginners' Kraut (page 178), to serve

* See Glossary

Trim the livers and remove any sinew. Rinse the livers under cold water, place on paper towel and pat dry to remove any excess moisture. Season lightly with salt and pepper.

Heat 2 teaspoons of the coconut oil or fat in a large frying pan over medium heat. Add the livers, making sure you do not overcrowd the pan, and cook for 40–60 seconds, or until nicely browned. Turn over and brown on the other side. Transfer the livers to a bowl and set aside to cool.

Add the onion and garlic to the pan with another 2 teaspoons of the oil or fat, season generously with salt and pepper and cook, stirring often, for 5 minutes, or until nice and brown. Stir in the paprika and bay leaf and cook for 30 seconds. Add the thyme and parsley and continue stirring for 20 seconds. Pour in the brandy (if using) and flambé (light the pan and allow the alcohol to cook out). Remove from the heat and set aside to cool.

Finely chop the livers, then return the livers to the bowl and add the remaining tablespoon of oil or fat and the stock. Stir through the onion and garlic mixture. Taste and add salt and pepper, if needed.

Transfer the livers to serving bowl and top with grated egg (if using). Serve with the crackers or bread and cultured carrots or kraut.

SERVES 4–6

These delicious chicken meatballs will be a hit at your next party. One thing I have learned over the years is that everything looks better and is received more lovingly if you make that extra bit of effort with presentation. A good trick is to buy organic chicken livers and freeze them in small quantities so you can grab a few at a time to add to meatball and mince recipes.

MEXICAN CHICKEN MEATBALLS WITH TOMATILLO SAUCE

600 g chicken mince

250 g chorizo sausage, finely chopped

100 g chicken livers, finely chopped

1 egg

½ teaspoon sea salt

¼ teaspoon freshly ground black pepper

2 tablespoons chopped coriander leaves

2 tablespoons coconut oil

12 baby cos lettuce leaves

1 avocado, thinly sliced

1 red capsicum, thinly sliced

1 Lebanese cucumber, thinly sliced

1 lime, cut into wedges

coriander leaves, to serve

TOMATILLO SAUCE

1 tablespoon coconut oil

1 onion, finely chopped

4 garlic cloves, crushed

500 g tomatillos*, husks removed, chopped

2 pinches chipotle chilli powder*

1 teaspoon ground cumin

250 ml (1 cup) chicken stock

1 tablespoon honey (optional)

½ teaspoon sea salt

½ teaspoon freshly ground black pepper

* See Glossary

To make the tomatillo sauce, melt the coconut oil in a large frying pan over medium heat, then add the onion and garlic and cook for 2–4 minutes, or until translucent. Stir in the tomatillo, chilli powder, cumin and stock, bring to the boil, then reduce the heat and simmer for 15 minutes, or until the tomatillo has broken down. Mix in the honey (if using), remove the pan from the heat and allow to cool. Transfer the sauce to a blender and blend until smooth. Season with salt and pepper. Set aside.

Preheat the oven to 180°C.

In a large bowl, combine the chicken mince, chorizo, chicken liver, egg, salt, pepper and chopped coriander. Use your hands to combine and shape the mixture into walnut-sized balls (you should make about 24). Place on a tray and set aside.

Heat the coconut oil in a large ovenproof frying pan over medium–high heat. Add the meatballs and fry for a few minutes until brown on all sides. Transfer the pan to the oven and bake for 5–7 minutes, or until the meatballs are cooked all the way through.

Meanwhile, pour the tomatillo sauce into a saucepan, cover and simmer for 20 minutes, stirring occasionally to prevent burning. Add a little more stock if needed.

Place the lettuce leaves on serving plates or in paper cones. Add some avocado, capsicum and cucumber and squeeze over some lime. Place a couple of meatballs on top and spoon over a good amount of tomatillo sauce. Squeeze on some more lime, if desired, and finish with some coriander leaves.

SERVES 6

Heart-warming and utterly delicious are the descriptions that spring to mind when I think about this gorgeous soup. It really helps to use a great chicken stock as your base, but if you don't have time you can simply use water and let the ham hock do its work – it permeates the entire soup to create the most amazing flavour. As always, search out a quality butcher that stocks pasture-raised pigs or jump online to find one that will deliver to you. I usually double or triple this recipe so that we have leftovers for a few days. I love having this soup for breakfast in the cooler months or to pop it in a thermos to take to work. Leftovers can also be frozen and stored for up to 3 months.

HAM HOCK SOUP

1 tablespoon coconut oil or other good-quality fat*

2 onions, chopped

1 smoked ham hock (about 1–1.2 kg)

2 garlic cloves, sliced

2 celery stalks, sliced

2 carrots, cut into 5 mm slices

3 litres chicken stock (to make your own, see page 86) or water

2 zucchinis, cut into 5 mm slices

300 g pumpkin, cut into 2 cm pieces

2 large handfuls of kale leaves, stalks removed, roughly chopped

sea salt and freshly ground black pepper

* See Glossary

Heat the oil or fat in a large saucepan over medium heat. Add the onion and cook, stirring often, for 3–5 minutes, or until soft. Add the ham hock, garlic, celery and carrot. Pour in the stock or water and bring to the boil. Reduce the heat to low, cover and simmer for 1½–2 hours, or until the meat is just falling off the bone. The ham hock needs to be completely submerged during cooking, so add a little more stock or water if necessary.

Add the zucchini and pumpkin to the pan and cook for a further 30 minutes, or until the zucchini and pumpkin are soft and the meat is falling off the bone.

Remove the ham hock from the soup and, when cool enough to handle, remove the meat from the bone, discarding the skin and fat. Shred or chop the meat and return to the pan. Stir in the kale and continue to cook until heated through. Season with salt and pepper.

Ladle the soup into warmed bowls and serve.

SERVES 8

Pulled pork is a dish made from the toughest and cheapest cuts that have been slow cooked until fork-tender. Here I team the pork with some paleo tortillas to keep everyone happy – we all love to wrap things up and eat with our hands. Please play around with secondary (cheaper) cuts from other animals like cow, lamb, venison or duck. This is a great lunch option the next day with a simple salad and some guacamole and fermented vegetables.

PULLED PORK TORTILLAS

1 kg boneless pork shoulder

3 tablespoons coconut oil or other good-quality fat*, melted

sea salt and freshly ground black pepper

3 tablespoons maple syrup

3 tablespoons garlic powder

½ teaspoon dry mustard powder

2 tablespoons onion powder

½ teaspoon ground white pepper

125 ml (½ cup) barbecue sauce (to make your own, see page 40)

125 ml (½ cup) Worcestershire sauce (to make your own, see page 206)

COCONUT FLOUR TORTILLAS

3 tablespoons coconut flour

3 tablespoons arrowroot*

¼ teaspoon baking powder

½ teaspoon fine sea salt

8 eggwhites from large eggs

2 tablespoons coconut oil

TO SERVE

Coleslaw with Chervil Dressing (page 172)

chipotle chilli powder*

barbecue sauce (to make your own, see page 40)

1 handful of coriander leaves

lime wedges

* See Glossary

Preheat the oven to 150°C. Lightly grease a roasting tin.

Trim the pork, rinse and pat dry with paper towel. Cut the pork in half, then rub with 1 tablespoon of the coconut oil or other fat. Sprinkle with salt and pepper.

Heat the remaining oil or fat in a large frying pan over high heat. Add the pork halves and sear for 2 minutes on all sides until lightly browned. Place the pork halves, fat side up, in the prepared tin. Mix the maple syrup, garlic powder, mustard powder, onion powder, barbecue sauce, Worcestershire sauce and 750 ml of water in a bowl. Pour over the pork, cover the pan tightly with a double layer of foil and roast in the oven for 1 hour. Reduce the temperature to 100°C and continue roasting for 6–7 hours, or until the pork is very tender. Remove the pork, reserving the liquid. Slice or shred the pork, adding some of the reserved liquid to moisten. Season with more salt and pepper if needed.

To make the coconut flour tortillas, whisk the coconut flour, arrowroot, baking powder, salt, eggwhites and 125 ml of water in a large bowl to make a smooth batter.

Melt 1 teaspoon of the coconut oil in a small frying pan over medium–high heat. Pour about 3 tablespoons of batter into the pan. Slightly tilt and swirl the pan to spread the batter into a thin tortilla, about 13 cm in diameter. Cook for a few minutes, or until golden brown, then flip and cook the other side until lightly golden. Transfer to plate and keep warm. Repeat until you have eight tortillas.

To serve, top each tortilla with some coleslaw and pulled pork, sprinkle over a little chipotle chilli powder, drizzle over some barbecue sauce and finish with the coriander and a squeeze of lime.

SERVES 4

Whenever anyone tells me the paleo way of cooking is too hard, or that they don't understand it, the first thing I ask is if they love a roast. A roast is one of the most enjoyable meals to cook at home. It is super easy, the kids absolutely devour it and we get to eat the leftovers the next day. It really is a set-and-forget type of dish that takes only 10–15 minutes to prepare – the rest is done in the oven. Roast pork is an absolute cracker (pardon the pun); there is simply something so irresistible about eating crisp, crunchy, delicious crackling. I love to serve this with vibrant sautéed greens (page 185).

ROAST PORK WITH APPLE SAUCE

3 tablespoons coconut oil or other good-quality fat*, melted

2 teaspoons fennel seeds

2 teaspoons sea salt

1.8 kg boneless pork loin or leg

4 long, thin carrots, halved lengthways

1 onion, unpeeled, cut into thick slices

400 ml chicken stock (to make your own, see page 86)

1 bay leaf

APPLE SAUCE
1½ tablespoons ghee*

3 granny smith apples, peeled, cored and sliced

1½ tablespoons honey (optional)

pinch of ground cinnamon

1 garlic clove, finely chopped

*See Glossary

Preheat the oven to 230°C. Grease a roasting tin with 1 tablespoon of the coconut oil or other fat.

Using a mortar and pestle, grind the fennel seeds to a coarse powder. Mix in the salt and set aside.

Gently pour 250 ml of boiling water over the pork skin and pat dry with a paper towel. Discard the water. Diagonally and horizontally score the skin with a sharp knife in straight lines 2.5 cm apart. Roll the pork loin up tightly and tie at regular intervals with kitchen string.

Put the carrots and onions in the roasting dish, then place the pork on top. Drizzle the pork skin with the oil or other fat and rub over the salt and ground fennel, covering the skin and the meat evenly.

Roast for 30 minutes, or until the pork skin is beginning to crackle. Reduce the temperature to 180°C, then add the chicken stock and bay leaf and continue to roast for 1 hour, or until the pork is tender and just cooked through. Cover with foil and let the pork rest for 15 minutes before carving.

Meanwhile, to make the apple sauce, melt the ghee in a frying pan over low heat. Add the apple and cook for 10 minutes. Stir in the honey (if using), cinnamon and garlic, cover and cook for 5 minutes, stirring occasionally, until the apple is soft. Puree the apple mixture in a blender or food processor. Set aside to cool.

Carve the pork into thick slices and serve with sautéed greens and the apple sauce.

SERVES 6–8

Cutlets are a bit of a luxury these days, as they have skyrocketed in price. If you'd prefer a different cut of meat, try fillets, backstraps or even brains and liver. I have teamed these little beauties with some capsicum relish and a simple salad to make a sensational dinner. These are also fabulous for the kids to take to school (just check on their school's nut-allergy policy first) or for the big kids to take to work.

CRUMBED LAMB CUTLETS WITH ROASTED CAPSICUM RELISH

200 g (2 cups) almond meal

2 teaspoons garlic powder

2 teaspoons onion powder

2 teaspoons dried parsley

60 g (½ cup) tapioca flour*

2 eggs

4 tablespoons almond milk

6 lamb cutlets, French-trimmed

400 ml coconut oil or other good-quality fat*, melted

lemon halves, to serve

2 tablespoons lemon juice

½ teaspoon wholegrain mustard or Fermented Mustard (page 177)

4 tablespoons extra-virgin olive oil

1 handful of rocket leaves

1 handful of mint leaves

½ fennel bulb, shaved

ROASTED CAPSICUM RELISH

2 red capsicums, quartered

2 tablespoons coconut oil

1 large onion, thinly sliced

1 garlic clove, finely chopped

1 teaspoon thyme leaves, finely chopped

sea salt and freshly ground black pepper

2 tablespoons red wine vinegar

1 teaspoon honey (optional)

*See Glossary

Preheat the oven to 200°C.

To make the roasted capsicum relish, place the capsicum, skin-side up, on a baking tray. Roast in the oven for 10–15 minutes, or until the skin blisters and blackens. Place the capsicum in a bowl, cover with plastic wrap and set aside to steam for 5 minutes. Peel off the skin and discard. Chop the capsicum. Heat the oil in a large non-stick frying pan over medium heat. Add the onion and garlic and cook for about 5 minutes, or until softened. Stir in the capsicum and thyme and season with salt and pepper. Reduce the heat to low and simmer for 20 minutes, then pour in the vinegar and honey (if using) and mix well. Taste and add a little more vinegar, if necessary. Cool.

Combine the almond meal, dried spices and herbs in a shallow bowl, season with salt and pepper and mix well. Place the tapioca flour in another bowl and whisk together the eggs and almond milk in a third shallow bowl.

Dust each cutlet in the tapioca flour, shake off the excess, then dip in the egg mixture and finally coat in a layer of almond meal crumbs.

Heat the coconut oil in a large frying pan over medium–high heat. When the oil reaches 160°C (a cube of bread dropped into the oil will turn golden brown in 30–35 seconds), shallow fry the cutlets (do not overcrowd the pan) for 2 minutes on each side until golden and cooked through. Remove from the pan and place on paper towel to soak up the excess oil. Season with salt and pepper. Allow to rest for 5 minutes before serving.

To make the salad, mix the lemon juice, mustard and olive oil in a bowl. In a separate bowl, combine the rocket, mint and fennel, gently toss through the dressing and season with salt and pepper.

Serve the lamb cutlets with the roasted capsicum relish, the rocket, fennel and mint salad and the lemon halves.

SERVES 2

Growing up on the Gold Coast, I spent most of my time at the beach learning to surf and fish. Afterwards, my mates and I would race to the bakery just down from the beach and eat pies with tomato sauce. We thought that life couldn't get any better! Transforming this pie into a healthy version was a really big deal for me. I have chosen to fill it with lamb shanks, but you could use lamb shoulder or beef, and add whichever veggies you love. The pastry is made from nut and coconut flour as well as pork fat, which is a better choice than the margarine and vegetable oil that is used in store-bought pastry.

LAMB SHANK PIE

2 tablespoons coconut oil or other good-quality fat*

4 lamb shanks, French-trimmed

sea salt and freshly ground black pepper

4 garlic cloves, crushed

2 carrots, chopped

1 onion, chopped

2 celery stalks, chopped

1 sweet potato, diced

1 × 400 g can whole peeled tomatoes

250 ml (1 cup) good-quality red wine

500 ml (2 cups) beef stock or water

2 tablespoons tapioca flour*

3 tablespoons chopped flat-leaf parsley leaves

4 thyme sprigs, leaves picked and chopped

good-quality tomato ketchup (to make your own, see page 72), to serve

SHORT PASTRY

100 g (1 cup) almond meal

100 g (¾ cup) coconut flour

60 g (½ cup) tapioca flour*

¾ teaspoon Himalayan salt

250 ml (1 cup) chilled lard*, ghee* or coconut oil

2 eggs

* See Glossary

Rub 1 tablespoon of the coconut oil or fat on the lamb shanks and season with salt and pepper. Place the shanks in a large saucepan or flameproof casserole dish over medium heat and brown on all sides for a few minutes. Drain off any excess oil and transfer the shanks to a warm plate.

Heat the remaining tablespoon of oil or fat in the same pan over medium heat and add all the vegetables. Increase the heat to high and cook, stirring occasionally, for 2 minutes, or until the vegetables begin to soften. Reduce the heat to medium and cook, stirring occasionally, for a further 15 minutes.

While the vegetables are cooking, place the tomatoes in a blender with the red wine, beef stock or water and tapioca, then blitz until combined.

Return the shanks to the pan or dish and pour in the blended tomato mixture (the meaty parts of the shanks should be well submerged). Cover and simmer gently over low heat for 2 hours, or until the shanks are tender. Stir occasionally to prevent from burning. Remove the shanks from the pan and place in a large bowl. When cool enough to handle, shred the meat from the bones and return the meat to the pan or dish. Bring to the boil, then reduce heat and simmer, uncovered and stirring occasionally, for 30 minutes until the mixture is thick. Taste and season with salt and pepper. Allow to cool completely before making the pie crust.

To make the short pastry, combine the almond meal, coconut flour, tapioca flour and salt in a bowl and mix well. Chop the lard into small dice and work into the flour mixture with your fingertips until a fine crumb-like texture forms. If using the ghee or coconut oil, place the almond meal, coconut flour, tapioca and ghee or oil in a food processor and process to fine crumbs, then transfer to a bowl. Add the salt and eggs to the crumb mixture and mix well to form a soft, sticky dough. Transfer to a lightly floured work surface and knead until smooth. Shape the dough into a ball, cover with plastic wrap and refrigerate for 2 hours, or until firm enough to roll out.

Recipe continued over page

LAMB SHANK PIE (cont.)

Preheat the oven to 160°C. Grease a 25 cm pie tin.

Divide the dough into two portions: one weighing 350 g, the other weighing 250 g.

Place the 350 g portion between two sheets of baking paper and roll out to form a circle about 4 mm thick and 30 cm in diameter. If the dough begins to crack slightly, simply bind it together by pinching the dough with your fingers and lightly smoothing out the areas where the cracks have formed.

Remove the top sheet of baking paper, invert the pie tin and place in the centre of the pastry round. Fold the edges of the baking paper around the pie tin and gently turn it right side up. Remove the baking paper. Press and smooth the pastry firmly into place ensuring that there are no gaps between the pastry and the tin. Fix any cracks by binding the dough together with your fingers. Trim the pastry edges using a sharp knife. Add the trimmed pastry to the remaining 250 g portion of dough.

Bake the pie shell in the oven for 8 minutes, or until lightly golden. Cool completely before adding the filling.

Meanwhile, on a sheet of baking paper, roll out the remaining portion of dough to form a 5 mm thick circle. Carefully transfer the pastry to a tray and refrigerate for 10 minutes until firm. Cut into a 25 cm round and return to the fridge until required.

Once the pie shell has completely cooled, fill with the lamb mixture. (Any leftover mixture can be stored in the freezer for later use.)

Remove the 25 cm pastry round from the fridge and carefully place on top of the filled pie shell, paper-side up. Gently run your fingers around the edge to seal, then carefully peel away the baking paper. Make an incision in the pastry lid by inserting the tip of a sharp knife directly into the centre of the pie (this allows the steam to escape while the pie is baking).

Bake for 30–35 minutes, or until golden and the filling is hot in the centre. If the pastry is browning too quickly, cover the top with some foil. Serve with the tomato ketchup.

SERVES 6

My girlfriend Nic and I love experimenting with curries, and my daughters, Chilli and Indii, are starting to appreciate the different spice combinations. Not all curries have to be hot; in fact, a lot don't have chilli in them, making them ideal for kids. Some curries are made with coconut milk or cream and some with stock. I tend to mix it up and sometimes use a mix of the two, as I have done in this recipe. Add as many different types of vegetable as you like or keep it simple and use one or two to really appreciate their flavour. As with all curries that use a secondary (cheaper and tougher) cut of meat, make sure you cook for a long time over a low temperature to make it fork-tender.

LAMB KORMA WITH CAULIFLOWER RICE

pinch of saffron threads

2 tablespoons coconut oil or ghee*

1 kg boneless lamb shoulder or leg, cut into 2.5 cm cubes

sea salt and freshly ground black pepper

1 onion, finely chopped

250 ml (1 cup) lamb or beef stock (to make your own, see page 84)

250 ml (1 cup) coconut milk

80 g (½ cup) cashews, ground (using a blender, food processor or mortar and pestle)

1 cinnamon stick

¼ teaspoon ground turmeric

¼ teaspoon sea salt

coriander leaves, to serve

Cauliflower Rice (page 180), to serve

GINGER AND GARLIC PASTE

5 cm piece of ginger, peeled and roughly chopped

6 large garlic cloves, chopped

¼ teaspoon sea salt

GARAM MASALA

8 cardamom pods, bruised

5 whole cloves

1 tablespoon coriander seeds

2 teaspoons cumin seeds

* See Glossary

To prepare the ginger and garlic paste, place the ginger, garlic and salt in a mortar and pestle, food processor or blender. Pour in 3 tablespoons of water and blend to a paste. Set aside until ready to use.

To prepare the garam masala, heat a frying pan over medium–high heat and add the cardamom pods and cloves. Heat for 30 seconds until fragrant but not burning, shake the pan and add the coriander seeds. Heat for 15 seconds, then add the cumin seeds. Heat for 15 seconds until all the spices are nicely fragrant. Transfer to a plate to cool, then grind to a powder using a spice grinder or mortar and pestle. Set aside.

Put the saffron in a small bowl and cover with 2 tablespoons of boiling water. Set aside to soak for at least 10 minutes.

Melt 1 tablespoon of the oil or ghee in a large saucepan over medium heat. Season the lamb with salt and pepper. When the oil or ghee is hot but not smoking, add the lamb in batches and brown for 1–2 minutes on each side. Try not to crowd the pan. Once the lamb is browned on all sides, remove to a plate.

Add the remaining oil or ghee to the pan with the onion, reduce the heat to medium–low and cook, stirring occasionally, for 5 minutes. Stir in the ginger and garlic paste and cook for 1 more minute. Add the garam masala, stir well and return the lamb to the pan with any juices that have accumulated on the plate. Stir well to coat the lamb with all the spices. Stir through the stock, coconut milk, ground cashews, cinnamon, saffron with its soaking water, turmeric and salt and bring to a low simmer. Cover and cook over low heat for 1½–2 hours, stirring occasionally.

Uncover the lamb korma, stir and, if necessary, cook for a few minutes until the sauce is reduced and thick. Season with additional salt and pepper. Remove the cinnamon stick, garnish with the coriander leaves and serve with the cauliflower rice.

SERVES 4–6

People can't resist these little morsels. I serve these cutlets with green beans and mint. Pure paleo folks eliminate all legumes from their diet, so feel free to replace the beans with zucchini, asparagus or broccoli.

LAMB CUTLETS WITH MINT SAUCE AND SAUTÉED BEANS

8 lamb cutlets, French-trimmed

salt and freshly ground black pepper

1 handful of mint leaves, to serve

MARINADE

1 large handful of flat-leaf parsley leaves

4 rosemary sprigs, leaves picked

100 ml coconut oil or ghee*, melted

5 garlic cloves

1 anchovy fillet

grated zest and juice of 1 lemon

MINT SAUCE

2 very large handfuls of mint, finely chopped

1 small garlic clove, crushed

½ French shallot, finely chopped

100 ml good-quality olive oil

1 tablespoon honey (optional)

2 tablespoons apple cider vinegar

2 pinches of ground cumin

BEANS

2 tablespoons coconut oil or good-quality fat*

2 large handfuls of green beans, sliced lengthways

2 garlic cloves, crushed

1 long red chilli, deseeded and finely chopped (optional)

4 tablespoons beef or lamb stock

extra-virgin olive oil, to serve

* See Glossary

For the marinade, place all the ingredients in a food processor and process to a coarse paste. Add more oil, if necessary.

Place the lamb cutlets in a large glass or ceramic dish. Rub the lamb with the marinade, season with salt and pepper and refrigerate for 2 hours to develop the flavours. Bring the lamb to room temperature before cooking.

Preheat the barbecue or chargrill hotplate to hot. Reduce the heat to medium and cook the cutlets for 2 minutes on each side for medium–rare, or until cooked to your liking. Transfer the cutlets to a tray, cover with foil and set aside for 5 minutes to rest.

To make the mint sauce, mix all the ingredients in a bowl, adding more oil, if necessary. Season with salt and pepper and set aside.

Meanwhile, for the beans, heat the oil or other fat in a large saucepan over high heat. Add the beans, garlic and chilli (if using) and sauté for 2–3 minutes, or until just tender. Pour in the stock and simmer for 3 minutes, or until the beans are tender and the stock has almost completely reduced. Season to taste, transfer to a serving bowl and drizzle with the extra-virgin olive oil.

Garnish the lamb cutlets with the mint leaves and serve with the sautéed beans and the mint sauce.

SERVES 4

If you ask a bunch of kids what their favourite home-cooked meal is, I guarantee at least half will say spaghetti bolognese. And don't even get them started on whose mum or dad makes it better, because that is some pretty heavy stuff. I have borrowed my mum's recipe and tweaked it to make it fit with the paleo way of eating. The pasta I have replaced with parsnip noodles. Feel free to use zucchini, celeriac, carrot or kelp noodles instead. It is up to you what type of mince you use. My mum uses a mixture of pork and beef. I have been using emu mince quite a lot lately – the kids think it tastes even better than the original!

CHILLI'S PARSNIP SPAGHETTI BOLOGNESE

3 tablespoons coconut oil

½ onion, finely chopped

3 garlic cloves, finely chopped

500 g beef mince

1 teaspoon dried oregano

250 ml (1 cup) red wine (optional)

2 tablespoons tomato paste

1 x 400 g can crushed tomatoes

250 ml (1 cup) chicken stock

Himalayan salt and freshly ground black pepper

6 parsnips, sliced into spaghetti strips on a mandoline

2 tablespoons olive oil

1 small handful of basil or flat-leaf parsley leaves, chopped

Heat 2 tablespoons of the oil in a large frying pan over medium heat. Add the onion and garlic and cook, stirring, for 5 minutes, or until soft. Add the beef and cook, stirring with a wooden spoon to break up any lumps, for 5 minutes, or until browned. Stir in the oregano and wine (if using) and cook until the wine has almost evaporated.

Stir the tomato paste into the beef mixture and cook for 1 minute. Add the tomatoes, half the stock and a good pinch of salt and pepper. Simmer, stirring occasionally, over low heat for 30 minutes, adding the remaining stock if the sauce is drying out.

Meanwhile, to make the parsnip spaghetti, bring a large saucepan of water to the boil. Add the parsnip strips and boil for 1 minute, or until tender. Drain.

Add the remaining tablespoon of coconut oil to a large frying pan and place over medium heat. Add the parsnip and cook for 1–2 minutes (the parsnip should not colour). Remove from the heat, toss through the olive oil and season with salt.

Divide the parsnip spaghetti between four serving bowls. Spoon over the bolognese sauce, sprinkle with the basil or parsley and serve with some veggies or a salad.

SERVES 4

TIP

I always add offal to bolognese, burgers and meatballs to make them even more nutritious (I usually go with about 10 per cent of the total meat quantity – in this recipe it would be 50 g offal and 450 g beef mince). Try using minced liver, heart, marrow or brain.

Let's make meatloaf the most popular recipe for the year. You can use this recipe as a starting point and then create your own meatloaf, taking inspiration from cuisines around the world. Experiment with herbs and spices and different proteins, and let your imagination run wild. I want to see your images on Instagram and Facebook with the headline 'I'm bringing meatloaf back!'. You might get a few weird comments from your mates, but I guarantee they will want the recipe once they've tried it.

MY MEATLOAF

8 rashers of bacon

800 g beef mince

3 tablespoons flaxseed meal*

4 tablespoons chopped flat-leaf parsley leaves

1 carrot, finely diced

1 zucchini, finely diced

2 celery stalks, finely chopped

1 large onion, diced

2 garlic cloves, crushed

2 eggs, lightly whisked

1 tablespoon Himalayan salt

½ tablespoon freshly cracked black pepper

2 tablespoons coconut oil or other good-quality fat*

125 ml (½ cup) coconut milk or almond milk (to make your own, see page 258)

4 tablespoons good-quality ketchup (to make your own, see page 72)

1 tablespoon honey (optional)

1 tablespoon apple cider vinegar

* See Glossary

Preheat the oven to 180°C.

Line the base and sides of a loaf tin with a piece of baking paper, cutting into the corners to fit and allowing the paper to extend 5 cm above the sides. Line the base and sides of the prepared tin with five slices of the bacon, reserving the remaining slices for the top.

Place the mince, flaxseed meal, parsley, carrot, zucchini, celery, onion, garlic, eggs, salt, pepper, oil or fat and coconut milk or almond milk in a bowl and mix until well combined.

Pack the meat mixture into the lined loaf tin, and then lay the remaining bacon slices over the top, tucking them in so that they won't overhang from the sides. Bake in the oven for 25 minutes.

Meanwhile, to make the glaze, mix the tomato ketchup, honey (if using) and vinegar in a small bowl.

Remove from the oven and baste the top with the glaze. Return to the oven and continue cooking for a further 25 minutes, or until cooked through. (To test if it's cooked, insert a thermometer into the meatloaf – it should reach 70°C.) Allow the meatloaf to rest in a warm place for 10 minutes before turning out from the tin. Slice and serve with your favourite salad or roasted veggies.

SERVES 8

My mum was the stir-fry queen when I was growing up. She would experiment with different proteins, such as chook, beef, lamb, pork, prawns or fish, and a multitude of vegetables to entice my growing tastebuds. I think she would often time stir-fry nights with when I went surfing after school, as I would return home ravenous and willing to devour anything put in front of me. I tend to do the same now with my girls. They love a good stir-fry and it is a great way to introduce new spices.

BEEF AND BROCCOLI STIR-FRY

400 g kelp noodles*

3 tablespoons coconut oil, plus extra if needed

600 g beef eye fillet, cut into strips

1 small onion, sliced

1 head of broccoli, broken into small florets

3 garlic cloves, sliced

4 shiitake mushrooms, chopped

4 oyster mushrooms, sliced

200 g bok choy, coarsely chopped

2 spring onions, thinly sliced

25 g (¼ cup) bean sprouts

1 carrot, julienned

1 zucchini, julienned

sea salt and freshly ground black pepper

chopped coriander leaves, to serve

TAMARI AND GINGER SAUCE

2 tablespoons apple cider vinegar

100 ml tamari

1 tablespoon honey (optional)

1 tablespoon grated ginger

1 teaspoon dried chilli flakes (optional)

1 teaspoon ground cumin

1 tablespoon fish sauce

* See Glossary

To make the tamari and ginger sauce, mix all the ingredients together in a bowl and set aside.

Rinse the kelp noodles under cold running water and set aside.

Melt the coconut oil in a wok or large heavy-based frying pan over high heat. Working in batches, sauté the beef until just brown (about 1 minute). Transfer to a plate.

Add more oil to the pan if necessary. Add the onion and garlic and stir-fry for 1 minute until just turning brown. Add the rest of the vegetables and stir-fry for a minute or so until they reach your preferred level of crunch. Return the beef to the pan. Pour in the tamari and ginger sauce, mix everything together and cook for 1 minute. Season with salt and pepper and mix in the coriander.

Divide the kelp noodles between four serving bowls and spoon over the stir-fry.

SERVES 4

This was the first pizza I perfected when, over a decade ago, I opened my first pizza restaurant. I wanted to create a pepperoni pizza that would stop people in their tracks. First, I found a pepperoni maker who was using pasture-raised rare-breed pigs and no preservatives. Second, I had to work out the best accompaniments. We all know that tomato is the queen flavour on the pizza, and the pig the king, so I just needed a court jester to liven up the party. I decided on chilli flakes and mint, which are an unusual but fabulous combination, as one is hot and the other is cooling. My daughter Indii is a huge fan of this pizza, or anything with sausage on it, for that matter! We cook this for the girls every month or so and they love coming up with their own flavour combinations.

INDII'S PEPPERONI PIZZA

1 Paleo Pizza Base (page 91)

4 tablespoons Pizza Sauce (page 63)

1 tablespoon chopped flat-leaf parsley leaves

6–8 cherry tomatoes, sliced

10 slices of pepperoni

100 g Cashew Cheese (page 218)

sea salt and freshly ground black pepper

2 macadamia nuts, finely grated

mint leaves, to serve

extra-virgin olive oil, to serve

Preheat the oven to 250°C or the highest temperature setting. If you have a pizza stone, heat it in the oven for 15 minutes. (If you don't have a pizza stone, you can use a baking tray, which does not require preheating.)

Prepare your pizza base as per the instructions on page 91. (You will cook one side of the base in the process.)

Spread the pizza sauce evenly over the pizza base, then sprinkle the parsley, cherry tomato slices, pepperoni and cashew cheese over the top and season with salt and pepper. Transfer the pizza to the hot pizza stone or a baking tray. Bake for 5–10 minutes until golden and crispy.

Sprinkle the grated macadamias over the top, garnish with the mint leaves, drizzle on a little olive oil and serve.

SERVES 1 REALLY HUNGRY PERSON

As a kid, I used to love coming home after a long surf and seeing my mum, Joy, making burger patties. Not a lot has changed since then. I still love going for long surfs and still feel starving afterwards. This recipe is basically the same as the one I grew up eating, but uses grilled mushrooms instead of a bread bun. If you don't like mushies, you could also use Seed and Nut Bread (page 23) or Egg Bread (page 24).

JOY BURGER

8 large portobello mushrooms

4 tablespoons coconut oil or other good-quality fat*, melted

Himalayan salt and freshly ground black pepper

4 rashers of bacon (optional)

2 onions, sliced into rings

4 eggs

8 slices of tomato

4 gherkins, sliced

2 carrots, grated

1 large beetroot, julienned

8 butter lettuce leaves

good-quality tomato ketchup (to make your own, see page 72), to serve

wholegrain mustard or Fermented Mustard (page 177), to serve

Chipotle Aioli (page 38), to serve

PATTIES

600 g chuck steak, minced

½ onion, finely diced

2 garlic cloves, crushed

1 egg

1 tablespoon Dijon or wholegrain mustard

pinch of dried chilli flakes

1 tablespoon chopped flat-leaf parsley leaves

pinch of dried oregano

1 teaspoon each of Himalayan salt and freshly ground black pepper

* See Glossary

Preheat the oven to 220°C. Line a baking tray with baking paper.

Destem the mushrooms and place them stem-side down on the tray. Drizzle on 1 tablespoon of the coconut oil or other fat, season with salt and pepper and bake in the oven for 10–15 minutes, or until the mushrooms are tender. Place the mushrooms on paper towel to remove excess moisture. Allow to cool.

Place all the patty ingredients in a large bowl and mix well. Shape into four patties.

Heat a barbecue hotplate to medium–high. Add 2 tablespoons of the coconut oil or other fat and cook the patties, bacon (if using) and onion for 5 minutes. Stir the onion occasionally so that it doesn't burn. Turn over the patties and bacon and continue to cook for a couple of minutes until the patties are cooked through, the bacon is crisp and the onion is caramelised. Remove from the barbecue and keep warm. Add the remaining tablespoon of coconut oil or other fat and cook the eggs to your liking. Season with salt and pepper.

Place the patties, mushrooms, onion, eggs and bacon (if using) on a serving platter in the centre of the table. Place the tomato, gherkins, carrot, beetroot, lettuce, tomato ketchup, mustard and chipotle aioli in bowls and let everyone build their own burger.

SERVES 4

Roast beef is a family favourite in many homes and rightly so. To be able to cook a nice slab of beef slowly and evenly without too much fuss is a double thumbs-up for me. What I love about roast beef is that it tastes great cold, and when you roast an eye fillet, sirloin, rib eye, chuck or rump, there is usually a lot left over for lunches the next day. I have teamed the roast with a paleo gravy here, which will keep the family happy; however, a simple salsa verde or pesto, or even some grated horseradish is a perfect accompaniment, too. Serve this with a big platter of roasted veg and you have a beautifully balanced meal.

ROAST BEEF AND GRAVY

1.2 kg rolled and hand-tied scotch fillet, boneless rib eye, sirloin or rump

4 tablespoons coconut oil or other good-quality fat*

sea salt and freshly ground black pepper

2 carrots, halved lengthways

1 onion, skin left on, thickly sliced

1 garlic bulb, cloves separated and peeled

8 sprigs of parsley, leaves picked and torn

4 sprigs of thyme

600 ml beef stock (to make your own, see page 84)

* See Glossary

Preheat the oven to 160°C.

Rub the beef with a little coconut oil or fat and a generous pinch each of salt and pepper. Heat 2 tablespoons of the coconut oil or fat in a large roasting tin over high heat. Cook the beef, turning occasionally, for 5 minutes, or until well browned on all sides.

Remove the beef from the roasting tin and add the carrot, onion and garlic in a single layer. Place the beef on top of the vegetables and add 250 ml of water. Roast for 60 minutes if you like your beef medium–rare (55–60°C using a meat thermometer) or for 65 minutes for medium (63–66°C). If you like your meat well done, leave in the oven for a further 10–15 minutes until it reaches 69–74°C.

Transfer the roast beef to a carving tray, cover loosely with foil and allow to rest for 15 minutes.

To make the gravy, discard the skin from the onion, pour in the beef stock and place the roasting tin over medium heat. Use a wooden spoon to scrape the base of the tin to dislodge any cooked-on bits. Add the thyme. Bring to the boil, reduce the heat to low and simmer, stirring occasionally, for 15 minutes. Season with salt and pepper. Skim and discard the layer of fat from the surface. Place the vegetables and liquid in a blender and blend until smooth, then pass through a fine sieve. If the gravy is too thin, transfer it to a saucepan and cook over medium heat until it reaches your desired consistency.

Cut the roast beef into thick slices, arrange the slices on serving plates and serve with roasted vegetables and gravy. Leftover gravy can be transferred to an airtight container and frozen for another time. It will keep for 3 months in the freezer.

SERVES 4–6

SIDES

It goes without saying that a daily salad is great idea, especially when the weather is warm. I wanted to include a very basic recipe for a garden salad in this book to remind people that simple is perfectly fine. We don't need to be super chefs every time we step foot in the kitchen, and sometimes cookbooks can make us feel a bit intimidated – and that goes for me, too. I buy cookbooks from the best chefs in the world and my jaw drops at the images and techniques. I view them as inspiration – I don't think I will ever try to tackle their recipes. My goal or job is to inspire you, offer encouragement and give you the best advice I can on feeding your family nutritious meals. Enjoy!

SIMPLE GARDEN SALAD

½ iceberg lettuce, leaves torn

6 button mushrooms, sliced

1 Lebanese cucumber, sliced

10 cherry tomatoes, halved

1 large carrot, sliced

3 radishes, thinly sliced

1 small handful of flat-leaf parsley leaves

DRESSING

185 ml (¾ cup) olive oil

100 ml apple cider vinegar

2 tablespoons lemon juice (optional)

1 teaspoon dried oregano

sea salt and freshly ground black pepper

To make the dressing, combine all the ingredients in a jar or bottle with a tight-fitting lid. Cover, shake well and chill.

Combine all the salad ingredients in a large serving bowl. Pour your desired amount of dressing over the top and toss to mix. Leftover dressing can be stored in a jar in the fridge for up to 2 days.

SERVES 4–6

Fermenting the humble carrot might be the easiest way to introduce fermented vegetables to your family. I think nearly every kid on the planet loves carrot, so the positive association is already there. Now all you have to do is tell them that these are super carrots, and watch their eyes light up. You might want to get them to draw a cartoon character of a super carrot or make up a song about the super carrot. Remember: never heat fermented veg as they lose their good bacteria. Serve them chilled or at room temperature. The fermented juice has so much goodness and can be combined with extra-virgin olive oil, herbs and seasoning to make a delicious salad dressing.

CULTURED CARROTS

1 teaspoon black peppercorns

6 large carrots, cut into 1 cm-thick batons

1½ teaspoons sea salt

1 sachet vegetable starter culture* (this will weigh 2–5 g, depending on the brand)

1 orange, zest peeled off in long strips

2 cinnamon sticks

1 small cabbage leaf, washed

* See Glossary

TIP

Because I love fermenting veggies so much, I have created a range of jars that are purpose-made to do exactly this. If you do use one of my Culture For Life fermentation jars, there is no need to cover and weight the vegetables with a folded cabbage leaf and a shot glass, as the jar has an in-built weighting system. There is also no need to cover with a tea towel, as there is a silicone cover provided to block out the light.

You will need a 1.5 litre preserving jar with an airlock lid for this recipe. Wash the jar and all the utensils you will be using thoroughly in very hot water or run them through a hot rinse cycle in the dishwasher.

Place the peppercorns in a small piece of muslin, tie into a bundle with kitchen string and set aside.

Place the carrot in a stainless steel bowl and sprinkle with salt. Mix well, cover and set aside.

Dissolve the starter culture in water according to the packet instructions (the amount of water will depend on the brand you are using). Add to the carrot along with the muslin bag containing the peppercorns, the orange zest and cinnamon sticks. Mix well.

Fill the prepared jar with the carrot, pressing down well with a large spoon to remove any air pockets and leaving 2 cm of room free at the top. The carrot should be completely submerged in the liquid, so add more water if necessary. Take the clean cabbage leaf, fold it up and place it on top of the carrot, then add a small glass weight (a shot glass is ideal) to keep everything submerged. Close the lid, then wrap a tea towel around the side of the jar to block out the light. Store in a dark place with a temperature of 16–23°C for 10–14 days. (You can place the jar in an esky to maintain a more consistent temperature.) Different vegetables have different culturing times and the warmer it is the shorter the time needed. The longer you leave the jar, the higher the level of good bacteria present. It is up to you how long you leave it – some people prefer the tangier flavour that comes with extra fermenting time, while others prefer a milder flavour.

Chill before eating. Once opened, it will last for up to 2 months in the fridge when kept submerged in liquid. If unopened, it will keep for up to 9 months in the fridge.

MAKES 1 × 1.5 LITRE JAR

I adored coleslaw as a kid and I didn't even know it had cabbage in it! Coleslaw is a very nutritious and versatile side dish – all you need to do is change the dressing to suit any cuisine. Please use this recipe as a guide and get the kids involved. Kids love a bit of creative licence and feel proud when they can lend a hand.

COLESLAW WITH CHERVIL DRESSING

3 beetroot, julienned

2 carrots, julienned

½ celeriac, julienned

1 kohlrabi*, julienned

1 large handful of thinly sliced fennel

¼ red cabbage, shredded

salt and freshly ground black pepper

2 large handfuls of mint leaves, shredded

2 handfuls of flat-leaf parsley leaves, roughly chopped

2 teaspoons finely grated lemon zest

CHERVIL DRESSING
juice of 2 lemons

3 tablespoons chopped chervil

125 g (½ cup) aioli (to make your own, see recipe below)

AIOLI
6 garlic confit cloves (to make your own, see below) or roasted garlic cloves

4 egg yolks

2 teaspoons Dijon mustard

2 teaspoons apple cider vinegar

2 tablespoons lemon juice

400 ml olive oil

salt and freshly ground black pepper

GARLIC CONFIT
25 garlic cloves, peeled

250 ml (1 cup) coconut oil

* See Glossary

Place the beetroot, carrot, celeriac, kohlrabi, fennel and cabbage in a large bowl and cover with cold water. Set aside while you make the dressing.

To make the chervil dressing, combine the lemon juice, chervil and aioli in a bowl and mix well.

Drain the vegetables and dry well with paper towel. Dry the bowl and replace the vegetables.

When ready to serve, add salt and pepper to taste, the herbs, lemon zest and chervil dressing to the vegetables. Toss well, pile onto plates and serve.

AIOLI

To make your own aioli, place the garlic, egg yolks, mustard, vinegar and lemon juice in a food processor and process until combined. With the motor running, slowly pour in the oil in a thin stream and process until the aioli is thick and creamy. Season with salt and pepper. Leftover aioli can be stored in an airtight container in the fridge for 4–5 days.

GARLIC CONFIT

To make the garlic confit, place the garlic cloves and coconut oil in a small saucepan over very low heat (you do not want to boil the oil). Cook for 2 hours, or until the garlic is beautifully soft. Leftover garlic confit can be transferred to a resealable jar with the oil and stored in the fridge for up to 3 months.

SERVES 6

My daughter Indii loves spicy food, whereas her older sister, Chilli, can't stand anything spicy (I think we got their names around the wrong way!). I have popped this recipe in the book as kimchi is a kick-ass dish, full of bioavailable nutrients. It makes a welcome addition to any Asian meal, or simply pop it on some fried or scrambled eggs for the best brekkie of your life. With fermented vegetables, always keep in mind that if you heat them, you start killing off the good bacteria. It is always preferable to eat them chilled or at room temperature.

KID-FRIENDLY KIMCHI

400 g red cabbage

400 g cabbage

100 g daikon (white radish), diced

1 green apple, cored and julienned

1 red onion, thinly sliced

1 French shallot, thinly sliced

1 handful of coriander leaves, chopped

juice of 1 lemon

1½ teaspoons sea salt

1 sachet vegetable starter culture*
(this will weigh 2–5 g, depending on the brand)

* See Glossary

▶ TIP

Because I love fermenting veggies so much, I have created a range of jars that are purpose-made to do exactly this. If you do use one of my Culture For Life fermentation jars, there is no need to cover and weight the vegetables with a folded cabbage leaf and a shot glass, as the jar has an in-built weighting system. There is also no need to cover with a tea towel, as there is a silicone cover provided to block out the light.

You will need a 1.5 litre preserving jar with an airlock lid for this recipe. Wash the jar and all the utensils you will be using in very hot water. Dry well and set aside. Alternatively, run them through a hot rinse cycle in the dishwasher.

Remove the outer leaves of the cabbages. Choose an unblemished leaf, wash it well and set aside for later. Shred the cabbages in a food processor or slice with a knife or mandoline, then transfer to a large glass or stainless steel bowl. Add the daikon, apple, onion, shallot, coriander, lemon juice and salt and mix well. Cover and set aside.

Prepare the starter culture according to the directions on the packet. Add to the vegetables and mix thoroughly.

Using a large spoon, fill the prepared jar with the vegetable mixture, pressing down well to remove any air pockets and leaving 2 cm of room at the top. The vegetables should be completely submerged in the liquid. Add more water, if necessary.

Take the clean cabbage leaf, fold it up and place it on top of the mixture, then add a small glass weight (a shot glass is ideal) to keep everything submerged. Close the lid, then wrap a tea towel around the side of the jar to block out the light.

Store the jar in a dark place with a temperature of 16–23°C for 10–14 days. (You can place the jar in an esky to maintain a more consistent temperature.) Different vegetables have different culturing times and the warmer it is the shorter the time needed. The longer you leave it, the higher the level of good bacteria and the tangier the flavour.

Chill before eating. Once opened, the kimchi will last for up to 2 months in the fridge when kept submerged in liquid. If unopened, it will keep for up to 9 months in the fridge.

MAKES 1 × 1.5 LITRE JAR

My partner Nic is the salad queen in our house and is always inventing new ways to spice them up. She'll take a simple salad like this and add some slowly toasted, spiced nuts and seeds to create another textural element. So feel free to use this salad as the starting point and add your own combination of nuts and seeds or even protein like smoked wild fish, leftover roast chicken or pork.

NIC'S CHOPPED SALAD

3 tomatoes, deseeded and diced

1 red capsicum, diced

1 long red chilli, deseeded and finely chopped

2 Lebanese cucumbers, diced

2 spring onions, thinly sliced

1 baby cos lettuce, chopped

80 g red cabbage, shredded

2 tablespoons chopped flat-leaf parsley leaves

2 tablespoons chopped coriander leaves

1 tablespoon chopped mint leaves

1 avocado, diced

40 g (¼ cup) pumpkin seeds

40 g (⅓ cup) sunflower seeds

DRESSING

1 teaspoon Dijon mustard or Fermented Mustard (see below)

2 tablespoons sherry vinegar

1 tablespoon lemon juice

4 tablespoons extra-virgin olive oil

salt and freshly ground black pepper

FERMENTED MUSTARD

185 ml sauerkraut brine (to make your own kraut, see page 178)

80 g mustard seeds

1 French shallot, finely chopped

2 garlic cloves, finely chopped

1 tablespoon maple syrup

sea salt

* See Glossary

To make the dressing, place the mustard, vinegar and lemon juice in a bowl and whisk to combine. Slowly add the oil in a thin, steady stream and whisk until incorporated. Season with salt and pepper.

Place all the salad ingredients in a bowl, add the dressing and gently toss. Season with salt and pepper. Allow the salad to stand for 10 minutes before serving.

FERMENTED MUSTARD

To make your own fermented mustard, you'll need a 250 ml preserving jar with an airlock lid. Wash the jar and all the utensils you will be using thoroughly in very hot water or run them through a hot rinse cycle in the dishwasher. Drain on a clean tea towel.

Combine the fermented brine liquid, mustard seeds, shallot and garlic in a glass or stainless steel bowl, cover with a plate and allow to soak at room temperature overnight.

The next day, combine the soaked mustard seed mixture with the maple syrup in a food processor. If you like lots of whole seeds in your mustard, you will only need to process for a short time; if you like a smooth mustard you'll need to process for longer. Store in the preserving jar in the fridge for up to 3 months.

SERVES 4–6

▶ **TIP**

You can use either brown or yellow mustard seeds in the fermented mustard recipe, or even a combination of both. Brown seeds are hotter and will make a spicier mustard.

Fermented vegetables will become a staple in homes over the next decade, not only because they taste amazing, but because of the scientific evidence coming out about how beneficial they are for our health. By including fermented vegetables in our diet, we are healing our second brain – our gut – and the truth of the matter is that many diseases originate in the gut, so the goal is to make the gut super healthy. One of the ways we can do this is by encouraging healthy bacteria. This child-friendly kraut is the perfect place to start – try adding half a teaspoon per meal and gradually build up to a tablespoon per meal and perhaps 2 tablespoons per meal for adults. It is super cheap to make and you might even become addicted to it.

BEGINNERS' KRAUT

400 g green cabbage

400 g red cabbage

1 beetroot, peeled

2 carrots (about 250 g in total)

1½ teaspoons sea salt

1 sachet vegetable starter culture*
(this will weigh 2–5 g, depending
on the brand)

* See Glossary

TIP

Because I love fermenting veggies so much, I have created a range of jars that are purpose-made to do exactly this. If you do use one of my Culture For Life fermentation jars, there is no need to cover and weight the vegetables with a folded cabbage leaf and a shot glass, as the jar has an in-built weighting system. There is also no need to cover with a tea towel, as there is a silicone cover provided to block out the light.

You will need a 1.5 litre preserving jar with an airlock lid for this recipe. Wash the jar and all the utensils you will be using in very hot water. Alternatively, run them through a hot rinse cycle in the dishwasher.

Remove the outer leaves of the cabbages. Choose an unblemished leaf, wash it well and set aside.

Shred the cabbages, beetroot and carrots in a food processor or slice with a knife or mandoline, then transfer to a large glass or stainless steel bowl. Sprinkle the salt over the vegetables, mix well and cover with a plate.

Prepare the starter culture according to the directions on the packet. Add to the vegetables and mix thoroughly.

Using a large spoon, fill the prepared jar with the vegetable mixture, pressing down well to remove any air pockets and leaving 2 cm free at the top. The vegetables should be completely submerged in the liquid. Add more water, if necessary.

Take the clean cabbage leaf, fold it up and place it on top of the vegetables, then add a small glass weight (a shot glass is ideal) to keep everything submerged. Close the lid and wrap a tea towel around the side of the jar to block out the light. Store in a dark place with a temperature of 16–23°C for 10–14 days. (You can place the jar in an esky to maintain a more consistent temperature.) Different vegetables have different culturing times and the warmer it is the shorter the time needed. The longer you leave the jar, the higher the level of good bacteria present. It is up to you how long you leave it – some people prefer the tangier flavour that comes with extra fermenting time, while others prefer a milder flavour.

Chill before eating. Once opened, it will last for up to 2 months in the fridge when kept submerged in liquid. If unopened, it will keep for up to 9 months in the fridge.

MAKES 1 × 1.5 LITRE JAR

CAULIFLOWER RICE

1 cauliflower, florets and stalk roughly chopped

2 tablespoons coconut oil

sea salt and freshly ground black pepper

Place the cauliflower in a food processor and pulse into tiny, fine pieces that look like rice.

Place the coconut oil in a large frying pan over medium heat. Add the cauliflower and lightly cook for 4–6 minutes, or until softened. Season with salt and pepper and serve.

SERVES 4

CELERIAC FRIES

4 tablespoons coconut oil, melted

800 g celeriac, cut into 5 mm thick strips

sea salt and freshly ground black pepper

Preheat the oven to 200°C. Lightly coat a large baking tray with a little of the coconut oil.

Place the celeriac and remaining coconut oil in a large bowl, season with salt and pepper and mix well. Spread on the prepared tray in a single layer. Bake for 10 minutes, then turn the celeriac strips over and continue to bake for another 5 minutes, or until tender and lightly browned. Keep a close eye on the fries as they can burn easily.

SERVES 4

BRUSSELS SPROUTS WITH BACON AND GARLIC

4 tablespoons duck fat*

200 g bacon, rind removed and roughly chopped

8 garlic cloves, thinly sliced

600 g brussels sprouts, chopped in half

* See Glossary

Heat the duck fat in a large, heavy-based frying pan over medium heat. Add the bacon and garlic and cook, stirring occasionally, for 4–6 minutes, or until lightly browned. Add the brussels sprouts and cook, stirring occasionally, for a further 10–15 minutes, or until the sprouts are tender when pierced with a fork. Serve.

SERVES 4

PUMPKIN MASH WITH COCONUT CREAM

500 g pumpkin, peeled and cut into 4 cm cubes

2 garlic cloves, peeled

2 tablespoons coconut oil or ghee*

125 ml (½ cup) coconut cream

sea salt and freshly ground black pepper

* See Glossary

Steam the pumpkin and garlic for 20–30 minutes, or until very tender.

Place the pumpkin and garlic in a blender, add the oil or ghee and half of the coconut cream and blend until very smooth. Season with salt and pepper. Drizzle the remaining coconut cream on top and serve.

SERVES 4

This is a hearty, luscious, satisfying accompaniment for just about any protein dish. I've used garlic and ginger for this mash, but you can add whichever spices you like to jazz it up. Try sprinkling it with fresh thyme leaves and a hint of cinnamon. One of my favourite ways to prepare and serve sweet spud mash is to add some freshly grated ginger and chopped coriander leaves and then team it with a piece of steamed fish and Asian greens. Remember that sweet potatoes are quite starchy, so if you are trying to lose weight or keep it off, go easy on them.

SWEET POTATO MASH

450 g sweet potato, peeled and cut into chunks

2 garlic cloves, peeled

125 ml (½ cup) coconut milk

1 tablespoon melted ghee* or extra-virgin olive oil

pinch of sea salt

freshly ground black pepper

1 teaspoon ground ginger

chopped coriander leaves, to serve

* See Glossary

Place the sweet potato and garlic in a saucepan, cover with cold water and bring to the boil. Reduce the heat to low, cover with a lid, and simmer for 20 minutes until tender. Drain the sweet potato and garlic, return to the pan and mash with a fork or a wooden spoon.

Add the coconut milk and ghee or olive oil to the sweet potato and mix until well combined. Stir through the salt, pepper and ginger, sprinkle over some chopped coriander leaves and serve immediately.

SERVES 4

There are countless inspiring recipes in this book, but the one that I'd most love to become a staple in your household is this one – humble green veg. I have deliberately kept this as simple as possible because the easier it is the more chance there is of making it to the dinner table. It's so important to eat green vegetables on a daily basis – and once you are in the habit of it, it's so easy to do. Peace, love and vegetables to you all!

SAUTÉED GREENS WITH LEMON AND GARLIC

1 bunch of broccolini (about 200 g)

6 asparagus spears, woody ends trimmed

1 handful of green beans

4 tablespoons coconut oil or other good-quality fat*

2 garlic cloves, finely sliced

½ bunch (about 200 g) of kale, stems removed, roughly chopped

2 zucchinis, thinly sliced on the diagonal

zest and juice of 1 lemon

sea salt and freshly ground black pepper

* See Glossary

Cut the stem ends off the broccolini and cut the tops in half.

Blanch the broccolini, asparagus and beans in boiling water for 2–3 minutes, or until just tender. Drain well.

Meanwhile, heat the oil in a large frying pan over medium heat. Add the garlic and cook for about 30 seconds, or until fragrant and starting to colour lightly. Add the zucchini and cook for 2 minutes. Add the broccolini, asparagus, beans and kale and sauté for 2 minutes, or until the veggies are just starting to crisp and turn golden. Remove from the heat. Stir in the lemon zest and juice and season to taste with salt and pepper, then serve.

SERVES 4

These sweet potato fries are super simple to make and are always a huge hit at any gathering. The best thing is that you can play around with flavour combinations to suit your own preferences – try cinnamon, thyme and sea salt; rosemary and garlic; or even sea salt and vinegar. These fries are roasted in the oven instead of being deep-fried – just make sure you give them a turn halfway through so they cook evenly.

SWEET POTATO FRIES WITH OREGANO AND SAGE

800 g sweet potato, cut into 5 mm thick strips

3 oregano sprigs, roughly chopped

10 sage leaves, roughly chopped

4 tablespoons coconut oil, melted

½ teaspoon sea salt

½ teaspoon freshly ground black pepper

Preheat the oven to 200°C. Lightly grease a large baking tray with a little coconut oil.

Combine the sweet potato, oregano, sage, oil, salt and pepper in a large bowl. Toss to mix well.

Spread the sweet potato fries on the prepared tray in a single layer. Roast in the oven for 10 minutes. Turn the fries over, then continue roasting for another 5 minutes, or until tender and lightly browned.

SERVES 4

VARIATION

You can use other herbs instead of the oregano. Try roughly chopped rosemary or thyme sprigs.

Roasted vegetables are one of our weekly staples. We always make a huge batch of them to go with our Sunday roast, as we adore the leftovers for breakfast, lunch, dinner or a snack. Leftover roast veggies can quickly be turned into a soup by adding some homemade stock and some protein. You can also whisk up some eggs, pour them over your chopped leftover veggies and bake the whole lot in the oven for a delicious frittata. Try adding some curry paste and coconut milk to the leftover veggies and you have a delicious roast vegetable curry. I like to eat leftovers straight out of the fridge, slathered in a simple dressing, topped with a good dollop of harissa or pesto or tossed with some leftover roast meat.

ROASTED VEGETABLES

2 parsnips, halved lengthways

1 onion, quartered

¼ jap pumpkin, cut into small wedges

200 g sweet potato, cut into 2 cm thick slices

2 carrots, sliced lengthways

1 garlic bulb, halved across the cloves

4 tablespoons coconut oil or other good-quality fat*, melted

sea salt and freshly ground black pepper

8 thyme sprigs

* See Glossary

Preheat the oven to 200°C.

Combine the parsnip, onion, pumpkin, sweet potato, carrot and garlic in a large roasting tin and toss with the oil or fat. Season with salt and pepper.

Spread the vegetables over the base of the tin to form a single layer, making sure they're not bunched up. Roast for 30–35 minutes, or until the vegetables are tender and golden. Garnish with the thyme and serve.

SERVES 4–6

SNACKS

I swear that every time I walk into a health food or organic store I am presented with a new flavour of bliss ball. They look delicious but they're pretty expensive, so why not make them at home? You can experiment with different spices, herbs, nuts, dried fruits, fresh fruit, vegetables, seeds and superfood powders. Eat them straight away or pop them in the fridge or freezer to create an icy cold treat for a summer's day.

STRAWBERRY BLISS BALLS

8 medjool dates, pitted

¼ banana, chopped

100 g (1 cup) walnuts (activated if possible, see page 200)

135 g (1 cup) chopped macadamia nuts (activated if possible, see page 200)

3 tablespoons coconut oil, melted

115 g (⅔ cup) chopped strawberries

3 tablespoons black or white chia seeds*

30 g (½ cup) desiccated coconut, plus extra for rolling

* See Glossary

Place the dates in a food processor and process until smooth. Add the banana, walnuts, macadamias, coconut oil, strawberries, chia seeds and coconut and pulse a few times until the mixture just comes together and the nuts have broken down to a crumb-like consistency but still have some texture.

Take a tablespoon of the mixture and roll into a walnut-sized ball with your hands. Roll the ball in the extra desiccated coconut and set on a plate or tray. Repeat until all the mixture has been shaped into small balls. Refrigerate for 20 minutes to set before serving. Store in an airtight container in the fridge for up to 1 week.

MAKES 18

Nut bars are considered a treat in our household so are not something that the kids eat daily. We take them on trips, to the movies (much better than popcorn) and hand them out at parties, as long as there are no guests with nut allergies. As with all the recipes in this book, play around with different ingredients that you and your family love and create your own super bar, or better yet, get the kids to make them with you.

NUT BARS

155 g (1 cup) almonds (activated if possible, see page 200)

100 g (1 cup) pecans (activated if possible, see page 200)

100 g (1 cup) walnuts (activated if possible, see page 200)

55 g (½ cup) almond meal

30 g (½ cup) shredded coconut

125 ml (½ cup) coconut oil

120 g (½ cup) almond butter

175 g (¼ cup) honey

½ teaspoon vanilla powder

¼ teaspoon sea salt

110 g (1 cup) dried cranberries, dried blueberries, raisins or goji berries (a mix of these is nice)

* See Glossary

Preheat the oven to 160°C. Line a deep baking tray with baking paper.

Place the almonds, pecans and walnuts on the baking tray and toast for 5 minutes, or until golden brown. Allow to cool. (If using activated nuts, you can omit this step, as it is already part of the activation process.)

Transfer the nuts to a food processor and pulse 4–5 times until coarsely ground. I like a coarse consistency as it adds a great texture.

Place the nuts in a large bowl, then stir though the almond meal and shredded coconut.

Melt the coconut oil and almond butter in a small saucepan over medium–low heat. Add the honey, vanilla and salt and mix well. Pour the honey mixture over the nuts, add the dried fruit and mix until well combined.

Spoon the nut mixture onto the prepared tray and smooth out using a palette knife or spatula. Refrigerate for 1–2 hours. Once set, cut into even-sized bars. Store in an airtight container in the fridge for up to 1 week.

MAKES ABOUT 10 BARS

DRIED FRUIT

4 tablespoons honey

juice of 1 lemon

1 apple, cored and thinly sliced

1 mango, thinly sliced

2 fresh figs, thinly sliced into rounds

6 strawberries, hulled and thinly sliced

Preheat the oven to 50°C or as low as it will go. Line two or three large baking trays with baking paper.

Place the honey and 125 ml of water in a small saucepan and bring to the boil, stirring occasionally. Remove from the heat and add the lemon juice. Allow to cool completely.

Dip the slices of apple in the syrup to coat, then place in a single layer on the prepared trays. Repeat with the mango, figs and strawberries. (The syrup prevents the fruit from discolouring.)

Bake for 7 hours, or until dry and crisp. Alternatively, use a dehydrator and follow the manufacturer's instructions. Allow to cool completely before serving or storing in an airtight container for up to 2 weeks.

SERVES 4

FRUIT ROLL-UPS

220 g dried figs (or other dried fruit, such as apricots, medjool dates, cranberries, raisins)

½ teaspoon ground cinnamon

2 tablespoons black or white chia seeds*

* See Glossary

Preheat the oven to 120°C. Line a baking tray with baking paper.

Combine the figs and 375 ml of water in a saucepan over medium heat. Bring to the boil and simmer for 20 minutes, or until the fruit is soft. Remove from the heat and drain the excess liquid.

Puree the fruit and cinnamon in a food processor until smooth. Pour onto the tray and spread evenly with a spatula, making sure there are no gaps or air bubbles. Sprinkle with the chia seeds and bake for 30 minutes. Turn off the oven and leave the tray in the oven for 8 hours, without opening the door.

Flip the roll up onto fresh baking paper, peel off the baking paper, roll the sheet into a log and cut into 12 pieces. Store in an airtight container in the pantry for up to 2 weeks.

MAKES 12

FRUIT KEBABS WITH COCONUT YOGHURT

¼ seedless watermelon, cut into 2.5 cm pieces

2 bananas, cut into 2.5 cm pieces

½ rockmelon, cut into 2.5 cm pieces

2 kiwifruit, cut into 2.5 cm pieces

12 strawberries, hulled

Coconut Yoghurt (page 16), to serve

shredded coconut, to serve

You will need 12 bamboo skewers for these kebabs.

Thread the fruit onto the skewers, alternating the fruit so that there is a variety on each skewer.

Serve with the yoghurt and shredded coconut. Kids will love dipping the kebabs into the yoghurt, then into the shredded coconut to coat, before gobbling them up.

MAKES 12

SEED CRACKERS WITH GUACAMOLE

Seed Crackers of your choice (page 204)

GUACAMOLE

1 avocado, diced

1 small red chilli, deseeded and finely diced

¼ red capsicum, finely diced

juice of 1 lime

1–2 tablespoons finely diced red onion

1 garlic clove, finely chopped

2 tablespoons chopped coriander leaves

1 tablespoon extra-virgin olive oil

To make the guacamole, combine all the ingredients in a small bowl.

Serve straight away with seed crackers of your choice and maybe some raw veg too.

SERVES 2–4

Trail mix is a combination of nuts, seeds and dried fruit. It is very easy to make and is a tasty snack to eat on the road, on planes, on long walks or hikes or to bring as part of a picnic. It offers a great source of usable energy for the whole body, which is what you need when you're exercising. Just how healthy your trail mix is really depends on the ingredients you use. Keep in mind that dried fruit will cause your blood sugar levels to rise, so I wouldn't advise eating too much of this on a regular basis, but from time to time you should be cool.

TRAIL MIX

40 g (¼ cup) almonds (activated if possible, see page 210)

30 g (¼ cup) pistachio nuts (activated if possible, see page 210)

40 g (¼ cup) cashews (activated if possible, see page 210)

35 g (¼ cup) hazelnuts (activated if possible, see page 210)

30 g (¼ cup) sunflower seeds

30 g (¼ cup) pumpkin seeds

8 dried apricots, chopped into small pieces

30 g (¼ cup) goji berries

20 g (⅓ cup) shaved coconut, lightly toasted

40 g (⅓ cup) dried cranberries or blueberries, or a mixture of both

Mix all the ingredients in a large bowl. Store in an airtight container for up to 3 months.

MAKES 375 G

Nuts are a wonderful source of good fats. In saying this, I wouldn't recommend eating large quantities on a daily basis, especially if you are concerned about your weight. As far as quantities go, a handful a day as a snack or in a salad is ideal. Nuts contain phytic acid, which when consumed binds to minerals such as iron, zinc, calcium, chromium, potassium and magnesium so that they cannot be readily absorbed. Activating the nuts – a simple process of soaking, then thoroughly rinsing them – lessens these phytates, making sure that we absorb as many of the good things as possible.

ACTIVATED NUTS

400 g raw nuts (such as almonds, macadamias, pecans, Brazil nuts, cashews)

2 teaspoons salt, garlic or onion powder, tamari or curry powder (optional)

Place the nuts in a bowl, add enough filtered water to cover, then set aside to soak. Hard nuts, like almonds, hazelnuts or Brazil nuts need to soak for 12 hours. Softer nuts, like cashews, macadamias or pecans only need 4–6 hours. After soaking, the nuts will look nice and puffy and may even start to show signs of sprouting.

Rinse the nuts under running water, and if you want to add flavour, now is the time to do it. Just shake your desired seasoning over the rinsed almonds, and stir well to coat.

Now, we want to toast the nuts without damaging all those nutrients we've activated. Either spread out on a baking tray and place in your oven preheated to the lowest temperature, about 50°C, or dry out in a dehydrator. This will take anywhere from 6 to 24 hours, depending on the temperature you're using. The nuts are done when they feel and taste dry.

Use your activated dried nuts as you would normally use toasted nuts. Store in an airtight container in the pantry for up to 3 months.

MAKES 400 G

> **TIP**

You can also make activated seeds using pumpkin or sunflower seeds. They need to be soaked for 6–8 hours, then simply proceed with the recipe as you would for the nuts.

This is a ripper of a recipe and it's guaranteed to get your kids wolfing down zucchini like there's no tomorrow. The best way to get kids to try new foods is to get them into the kitchen to help with the preparation – they want to see and taste their handiwork. Being able to pick some zucchinis from your garden or a friend's garden would really seal the deal! The spiced seasoning adds a lovely kick to these – just go easy on it if your kids aren't into spice.

ZUCCHINI CHIPS WITH HERB AIOLI

1 egg

125 ml (½ cup) almond milk (to make your own, see page 258)

50 g (½ cup) arrowroot*

100 g (1 cup) almond meal

2 large zucchinis, cut into 7.5 cm batons, about 1 cm thick

300 ml refined or unscented coconut oil

HERB AIOLI

1 tablespoon finely chopped flat-leaf parsley leaves

½ teaspoon finely grated lemon zest

250 g aioli (to make your own, see page 172)

SPICED SEASONING

3 tablespoons sea salt

2 tablespoons paprika

1 tablespoon garlic powder

1 teaspoon ground cumin

1 teaspoon ground white pepper

½ teaspoon chilli powder

½ teaspoon celery salt

* See Glossary

To make the spiced seasoning, combine all the ingredients in a small bowl and stir well. Set aside until ready to use.

To make the herb aioli, place the ingredients in a bowl and mix well. Refrigerate until required.

Whisk the egg in a bowl with the almond milk until well combined.

Place the arrowroot and almond meal into two small, shallow bowls.

Individually coat each zucchini stick in the arrowroot, shaking off any excess. Dip the coated zucchini in the egg mixture then roll in the almond meal, ensuring it is coated evenly. If you miss some patches, simply dab a little more egg mixture onto the dry areas and coat again with the almond meal.

Heat the coconut oil in a large, deep frying pan over medium heat. Test if the oil is hot enough by dropping in a small piece of zucchini – if the oil begins to bubble around the zucchini, it has reached the ideal temperature. Add the zucchini chips in batches, and cook for 2 minutes on each side, or until golden brown and crisp. Remove the chips from the pan using metal tongs or a slotted spoon, and transfer to paper towel to drain. Allow the chips to cool slightly before serving.

Sprinkle with a little spiced seasoning and serve with herb aioli. The leftover spiced seasoning can be stored in an airtight container in the pantry for several months.

SERVES 4

I think it is in our DNA to love crunchy and crispy things. Any time I've used those words to describe a dish on a menu, it's flown out the door. So I felt inspired to include one of my favourite crispy paleo snacks in this book. I have to admit that my gorgeous partner, Nic, is the master at making seed crackers in our house, and she is always playing around with different vegetables and spices. I don't think I have ever had the same ones twice and I love her creativity in the kitchen. These are perfect with any kind of dip (pages 217–219) and Wise Sons' Chopped Liver (page 134), or you can even crush them into small pieces and sprinkle over a salad or eggs.

NIC'S SEED CRACKERS

160 g flaxseeds*

80 g mixed seeds (such as pumpkin seeds, sunflower seeds, sesame seeds)

½ teaspoon sea salt

1 teaspoon of your favourite spice (such as cayenne pepper, smoked paprika, cumin seeds or fennel seeds)

See Glossary

Place the flaxseeds in a bowl with enough water to cover. Cover with a tea towel and leave to soak overnight. Place the mixed seeds in a separate bowl and pour over enough water to cover. Cover with a tea towel and leave to soak overnight.

The next morning, drain and rinse the flaxseeds and mixed seeds and combine in a blender. Add the salt and spice and pulse a few times to break up the seeds (but do not over-process; you want the seeds to be chopped but a little chunky).

Preheat the oven to 50°C or as low as it will go. Line 2 large baking trays with baking paper.

Spread the seed mixture very thinly on the trays. Bake for about 6 hours, turning over after 3 hours, until crisp and dry.

Cut or break the crackers into pieces. Store in an airtight container for 2–4 weeks.

SERVES 6–8

VARIATIONS

Seaweed and seed crackers
Follow the recipe above, substituting 1 tablespoon spirulina powder* and 1 tablespoon dried dulse flakes* for the spice.

Curry and seed crackers
Follow the recipe above, substituting 1½ tablespoons curry powder and 1 teaspoon garlic powder for the spice.

Sun-dried tomato and Italian herb crackers
Drain 12 sun-dried tomatoes packed in olive oil, and pat dry. Process in a food processor until smooth. Follow the recipe above, substituting 1 teaspoon mixed Italian herbs, 1 teaspoon garlic powder and the blended sun-dried tomatoes for the spice.

Jerky is a wonderful snack to have on hand for kids' lunchboxes, when guests pop over or to eat on car trips and plane rides. We make it in a dehydrator, a handy piece of equipment to have at home. Play around with the seasonings you use on the jerky and take inspiration from any cuisines around the globe.

BEEF JERKY

800 g flank or skirt steak

MARINADE

170 ml (⅔ cup) Worcestershire sauce (to make your own, see recipe below)

170 ml (⅔ cup) tamari

1 tablespoon honey (optional)

2 teaspoons freshly ground black pepper

2 teaspoons onion powder

1 teaspoon liquid smoke* (optional)

WORCESTERSHIRE SAUCE

250 ml (1 cup) apple cider vinegar

100 ml coconut aminos* or tamari

1 teaspoon ground ginger

1 teaspoon mustard powder

1 teaspoon onion powder

1 teaspoon garlic powder

½ teaspoon ground cinnamon

½ teaspoon freshly ground black pepper

* See Glossary

Trim the steak of any excess fat. Place the steak in the freezer for 1–2 hours to firm up.

Remove the steak from the freezer and thinly slice with the grain into long strips.

Combine the steak and the marinade ingredients in a large resealable bag. Seal and shake to evenly distribute the marinade, then place in the fridge for 3–6 hours.

Preheat the oven to 50°C. Line two large baking trays with baking paper.

Remove the steak from the fridge and shake of the excess marinade. Place the steak on the prepared trays in a single layer, making sure that the strips are not touching.

Place in the oven and cook for 8–12 hours, or until the meat is completely dry and slightly crisp. Alternatively, use a dehydrator and follow the manufacturer's instructions.

Once dry, store in an airtight container in a cool, dry place for 2–3 months.

WORCESTERSHIRE SAUCE

To make your own Worcestershire sauce, combine all the ingredients with 4 tablespoons of water in a small saucepan and bring to the boil over medium heat. Reduce the heat to low and simmer for 10–15 minutes, or until slightly thickened. Allow to cool before using. Leftover Worcestershire sauce can be stored in an airtight container in the fridge for up to 2 months.

SERVES 8

Savoury muffins are just as enjoyable as sweet muffins, especially since you are getting some veggies with each bite. In saying that, though, I wouldn't recommend a week-long binge on any of the muffins or desserts in this book. A pumpkin muffin or paleo dessert is fine from time to time, but it's best not to overdo it.

PUMPKIN MUFFINS

570 g grated pumpkin

5 eggs

¾ teaspoon sea salt

½ teaspoon garlic powder

½ teaspoon onion powder

2 pinches of ground nutmeg

¼ teaspoon ground ginger

¼ teaspoon freshly ground black pepper

3 tablespoons coconut oil or ghee*, melted

300 g (3 cups) almond meal

1½ tablespoons baking powder

1 tablespoon pumpkin seeds

1 tablespoon sunflower seeds

* See Glossary

Preheat the oven to 160°C. Grease a 12-hole muffin tin with coconut oil.

Combine the pumpkin, eggs, salt, garlic powder, onion powder, nutmeg, ginger, pepper and coconut oil or ghee in a large bowl. Add the almond meal and baking powder and mix well.

Spoon the mixture into the muffin tin and sprinkle the top with the pumpkin and sunflower seeds. Bake for 20–30 minutes, or until a skewer inserted into the centre of a muffin comes out clean. Remove from the oven and cool slightly before eating.

The muffins can be stored in an airtight container in the fridge for up to 4 days.

MAKES 12

Seriously, if you have never tried a kale chip, you are missing out. We devour them a couple of times a week and are always experimenting with flavours by using spices, herbs, nuts and seeds. The key here is to make enough for the whole family to enjoy. Trust me on this one, they don't last long. They are wonderful to eat by themselves, but try using them in salads or as a garnish for soups or braises. And for a bit of a colour and flavour explosion, there are also these delicious, crispy beetroot chips.

BEETROOT AND KALE CHIPS

KALE CHIPS

300 g kale

1 tablespoon coconut oil, melted

sea salt or Himalayan salt

BEETROOT CHIPS

3 beetroot

2 tablespoons coconut oil, melted

sea salt or Himalayan salt

Kale chips

Preheat the oven to 120°C. Line two large baking trays with baking paper.

Wash the kale thoroughly and pat dry. Remove and discard the tough ribs from the kale leaves, then cut the leaves into smaller pieces.

In a large bowl, toss the kale with the coconut oil and some salt – go easy on the salt as a little goes a long way.

Place the kale on the trays in a single layer, do not overcrowd. Roast in the oven until crispy, about 35–40 minutes. Serve at once or store in an airtight container in the pantry for up to 2 weeks.

SERVES 2–4

Beetroot chips

Preheat the oven to 140°C. Line three or four large baking trays with baking paper.

Peel the beetroot and cut into 2 mm thick slices with a mandoline. (If you don't have a mandoline, simply slice thinly with a sharp knife.)

Place the beetroot slices in a large bowl and, wearing gloves (because your hands will turn red otherwise), gently toss with the oil and season with salt.

Arrange a single layer of beetroot slices on the trays and bake for 15–20 minutes. Rotate the trays and cook for a further 10 minutes until the beetroot has lightened in colour and is crisp at the edges. Remove from the oven. The beetroot chips will crisp up as they cool. Store in an airtight container in the pantry for up to 2 weeks.

SERVES 2–4

I have the brilliant chef Ravi Kapur, one of the up-and-coming culinary magicians from San Francisco, to thank for showing me how to make crispy nori chips to use as a base for smoked trout dip. They are also awesome with some fresh tuna tartare. I served these chips at Christmas last year and they were an absolute hit with the whole family.

NORI CHIPS WITH SMOKED TROUT DIP

200 g smoked trout, bones removed, finely chopped

100 g Cashew Cheese (page 218)

1 red Asian shallot, finely diced

2 tablespoons lemon juice

60 g (¼ cup) mayonnaise (to make your own, see page 58)

sea salt and freshly ground black pepper

2 tablespoons trout roe

NORI CHIPS

150 g (1½ cups) tapioca flour*

150 ml ice-cold soda water

coconut oil, melted, for frying

3 nori sheets*, each one cut into 6 squares

sea salt

* See Glossary

To make the trout dip, place the trout, cashew cheese, shallot, lemon juice, mayonnaise and 2 tablespoons water in a food processor and blend until smooth. Season with salt and pepper.

Using a spatula, pass the trout mixture through a fine sieve so you have a smooth beautiful dip (and no unwanted bones). Refrigerate until ready to serve.

To make the nori crisps, place the tapioca flour in a bowl and slowly pour in the soda water while you whisk. Continue whisking until the batter has the consistency of pouring cream.

Add melted coconut oil to a depth of 10 cm to a wok or saucepan and place over high heat until it reaches about 160°C. (To test, drop a small piece of nori into the oil – if it starts bubbling straight away, it is ready.)

Dip each nori square, one at a time, into the batter to coat completely, then slide it straight into the hot oil. (The nori sheet will become soft very quickly once it is covered in the batter, so it's best to put it straight into the oil after coating.) Fry the battered nori in batches, cooking on each side for 20–30 seconds, or until light and golden. Drain on paper towel and sprinkle with salt.

Transfer the dip to a bowl, scatter over the trout roe and serve with the nori chips. Any leftover nori chips can be stored in an airtight container in the pantry for up to 3 days.

SERVES 4–6

Parsnip chips are a fun snack to add to your repertoire of crispy, crunchy delicacies. Vegetable chips give you an opportunity to introduce your family to different ingredients that they might usually refuse. We have had great success introducing kale, beetroot, parsnip, sweet potato and brussels sprouts into the kids' diet by first letting them try the chip versions.

PARSNIP CHIPS

2 parsnips, cut into 1 mm slices with a mandoline

125 ml (½ cup) coconut oil or other good-quality fat*, melted

SEASONING

¼ teaspoon garlic powder

¼ teaspoon onion powder

1 teaspoon sea salt

* See Glossary

Preheat the oven to 160°C. Line two or three large baking trays with baking paper.

To make the seasoning, combine all of the ingredients in a bowl.

Arrange the parsnip in a single layer on the prepared trays, brush with the olive oil and sprinkle on the seasoning. Bake in the oven for 6 minutes, flip and move the parsnip chips around to avoid uneven cooking, and continue to bake for another 6 minutes, or until golden and crispy.

SERVES 2–4

Spinach and artichoke dip

Roasted carrot hummus

Beetroot dip

See recipe on page 212

Smoked trout dip

Kale and tahini dip

Cashew cheese

MEDLEY OF DIPS

Gotta love dips, especially when they look and taste like these. You don't need
to follow these recipes exactly; rather you can use them as a starting point and
tweak as you go. Team these with Seed Crackers (page 204) and raw carrots, celery
and radish (my favourites), but also try okra, as it is heavenly eaten raw.

Beetroot dip

2 beetroot (500 g in total), scrubbed and trimmed

3 tablespoons extra-virgin olive oil

1 tablespoon pomegranate molasses*

4 garlic confit cloves (to make your own, see page 172) or roasted garlic cloves

½ teaspoon ground cumin

½ teaspoon ground coriander

sea salt and freshly ground black pepper

* See Glossary

Preheat the oven to 200°C.

Cut the beetroot in half, then wrap in foil and place on a baking tray. Bake for 40–60 minutes, or until tender when pierced with the tip of a small sharp knife. Remove from the oven and cool in the foil for 15 minutes.

When warm enough to handle, use gloves to peel the skin from the beetroot (the beetroot stains your hands and is a little tricky to rinse off).

Combine the beetroot with the oil, pomegranate molasses, garlic, cumin, coriander and 2 tablespoons of water in a food processor and blend until smooth. Season with salt and pepper and serve. The beetroot dip will keep in an airtight container in the fridge for up to 5 days.

MAKES 540 G

MEDLEY OF DIPS (cont.)

Cashew or macadamia cheese

320 g cashews or macadamia nuts

1–1½ tablespoons lemon juice

1 teaspoon sea salt

pinch of freshly ground black pepper

Soak the cashews or macadamias in 750 ml of water for 6 hours. Drain and rinse well.

Place the nuts in a food processor with the lemon juice, salt and pepper and pulse for 1 minute to combine. Add 120 ml of water and continue to process until smooth. If the cheese seems overly thick or dry, gradually add more water and lemon juice to adjust the consistency. You may need to add more water if using macadamia nuts instead of cashews. The nut cheese can be stored in an airtight container in the fridge for up to 1 week.

MAKES 600 G

Roasted carrot hummus

600 g carrots, cut into 2.5 cm pieces

½ teaspoon ground cumin

Himalayan salt and freshly ground black pepper

2 tablespoons coconut oil or other good-quality fat*, melted

4 garlic confit cloves (to make your own, see page 172) or roasted garlic cloves

3 tablespoons unhulled tahini

1 teaspoon finely grated ginger

3 tablespoons lemon juice

4 tablespoons extra-virgin olive oil

See Glossary

Preheat the oven to 190°C.

Place the carrot in a single layer in an oiled roasting tin. Sprinkle with the ground cumin, salt and pepper and drizzle over the coconut oil or other fat. Mix with your hands to coat well and roast in the oven for 20 minutes or until nicely coloured. Pour in 250 ml of water, cover with foil and roast in the oven for a further 35 minutes, or until the carrot is very tender. Allow to cool.

Place the carrot and all the cooking juices in a food processor and process until smooth. Add the garlic, tahini, ginger, lemon juice and olive oil and whiz until smooth. Add more water if needed. Season with salt and pepper and serve. The carrot hummus will keep in an airtight container in the fridge for up to 5 days.

MAKES 540 G

Spinach and artichoke dip

1 tablespoon coconut oil or other good-quality fat*

2 garlic cloves, chopped

100 g baby spinach leaves

sea salt and freshly ground black pepper

150 g artichoke hearts in brine, drained and finely chopped

100 g (½ cup) Cashew Cheese (page 218)

1 tablespoon lemon juice

3 tablespoons olive oil

½ teaspoon onion powder

* See Glossary

Melt the coconut oil or fat in a large frying pan over medium heat. Add the garlic and cook for 1 minute, or until fragrant, then stir in the spinach and sauté until wilted. Remove from the heat, season with salt and pepper and allow to cool.

Drain any excess liquid from the spinach and place in a food processor along with the remaining ingredients. Process until smooth, or if you like it a little chunky, process until you have reached the desired consistency. Season with salt and pepper and serve. The spinach dip will keep in an airtight container in the fridge for up to 5 days.

MAKES 320 G

Kale and tahini dip

1 tablespoon coconut oil

1 onion, diced

4 garlic cloves, minced

1 bunch of kale, central stalks removed, leaves chopped (you should be left with about 250 g leaves)

120 g (½ cup) unhulled tahini

100 ml extra-virgin olive oil

pinch of cayenne pepper (optional)

4 tablespoons freshly squeezed lemon juice

50 g (⅓ cup) macadamia nuts (activated if possible, see page 200)

sea salt and freshly ground black pepper

Melt the coconut oil in a large saucepan over medium heat. Add the onion and cook, stirring, for about 5 minutes, or until softened. Add the garlic and cook for about 30 seconds, or until it starts to colour. Add the kale and 125 ml water. Cover and cook for about 3 minutes, or until the kale is tender. Leave to cool slightly.

Transfer the kale mixture and the cooking liquid to a food processor and add the tahini, olive oil, cayenne pepper (if using), lemon juice, macadamia nuts, salt and pepper. Process until smooth and serve. The kale dip will keep in an airtight container in the fridge for up to 5 days.

MAKES 630 G

SWEETS

One of the best tips I have is to freeze overly ripe bananas to use for a rainy day. The key is to peel them, cut them into bite-sized pieces and pop them into a container to freeze. We use them to make dairy-free ice cream by blending them or putting them through our juicer (which has a homogenising cone to make them lovely and smooth). Other ways to use them are in pancake batters or in a banana bread recipe like this one.

BANANA BREAD

250 ml (1 cup) coconut oil, melted, plus extra for greasing

75 g (¾ cup) coconut flour

75 g (¾ cup) almond meal

1 teaspoon ground cinnamon

2 teaspoons baking soda

pinch of sea salt

5 very ripe bananas

6 eggs

¼ teaspoon vanilla powder

4½ tablespoons honey, plus extra for brushing

Preheat the oven to 160°C. Grease a 20 cm × 12 cm loaf tin with a little coconut oil, then line the base and sides with baking paper.

In a large bowl, combine the coconut flour, almond meal, cinnamon, baking soda and salt and mix well.

Place 4½ of the bananas in a bowl and mash thoroughly. Slice the remaining half banana diagonally into three or four pieces. Set aside.

In another bowl, whisk together the eggs, vanilla and honey, then stir in the mashed banana.

Pour the liquid ingredients into the dry ingredients and stir with a wooden spoon until thoroughly combined. Add the coconut oil and continue stirring until incorporated.

Spoon the batter into the prepared loaf tin and spread out evenly with a spatula. Arrange the banana slices on top. Bake in the oven for 15 minutes then cover with foil to prevent the top burning and cook for a further 45–50 minutes, or until a skewer inserted in the centre comes out clean.

Remove the bread from the oven and cool in the tin for 10 minutes, then carefully turn out onto a wire rack. Brush a little extra honey over the top and cool for 20–30 minutes. Slice and serve toasted spread with some coconut oil or almond butter.

MAKES 1 LOAF

I love creating recipes that will encourage the kids to get involved in the kitchen. Although I usually recommend their involvement in preparing savoury dishes, making and decorating gingerbread men is a great way to explain why you are using paleo alternatives instead of the usual ingredients.

GINGERBREAD MEN

¼ teaspoon bicarbonate of soda

½ teaspoon ground cinnamon

½ teaspoon ground cloves

½ teaspoon ground ginger

½ teaspoon freshly grated nutmeg

large pinch of sea salt

400 g (4 cups) almond meal

125 ml (½ cup) molasses

4 tablespoons maple syrup

125 ml (½ cup) coconut oil, melted

White Icing (page 280)

Preheat the oven to 160°C. Line two large baking trays with baking paper.

Combine all the dry ingredients in a large bowl.

In another bowl, combine the molasses, maple syrup and coconut oil. Stir the molasses mixture through the dry ingredients to form a soft and sticky dough. Place in the fridge for 1 hour to firm up.

Remove the dough from the fridge and place it between two sheets of baking paper. Roll out to 3 mm thick. Cut out gingerbread men shapes or shapes of your choice with lightly floured cookie cutters. Place on the prepared trays and bake for 8 minutes, or until golden brown.

Allow the gingerbread men to cool on the tray before decorating with the white icing.

MAKES 14 GINGERBREAD MEN

This is a great little recipe to make for celebrations or kids' birthday parties (make sure there are no nut allergies first). It is completely free of gluten, refined sugar and dairy. Again, as with all the desserts and treats in this book, just because it is paleo doesn't mean it should be part of your daily diet – view it as something to be enjoyed in moderation. These muffins are flavoured with carrot and apple; however, feel free to try grated beetroot or pear, goji berries or any other ingredients you have on hand.

APPLE AND CARROT MUFFINS

240 g (2⅓ cups) almond meal

60 g (½ cup) tapioca flour*

½ teaspoon maca powder* (optional)

1 tablespoon baking powder

¼ teaspoon Himalayan salt

115 g (⅓ cup) honey

60 ml (¼ cup) coconut oil, at room temperature

½ teaspoon vanilla powder

½ teaspoon freshly grated nutmeg

3 eggs

125 ml (½ cup) nut milk (to make your own, see page 258)

1 green or red apple, cored and grated

2 small carrots, grated

honey, to serve (optional)

shredded coconut, to serve

* See Glossary

Preheat the oven to 180°C. Line eight holes of a muffin tin with paper cases.

Combine the almond meal, tapioca flour, maca powder, baking powder and salt in a bowl and, using a fork, mash any clumps to make a fine mixture.

Using an electric mixer on medium speed, beat the honey and oil or ghee together until well creamed (about 4–5 minutes). Add the vanilla, nutmeg and eggs and beat for a further 2–3 minutes. Add the flour mixture and beat to combine, then slowly pour in the nut milk and mix well. Turn off the mixer and gently fold in the apple and carrot.

Divide the batter among the paper cases and bake for 25–30 minutes until the tops are starting to brown and a toothpick or metal skewer inserted in the centre of a muffin comes out clean.

Allow the muffins to cool in the tin for 3–5 minutes, then transfer to a wire rack to cool completely before serving. To serve, brush with some honey (if desired) and scatter over shredded coconut. The muffins can be stored in an airtight container in the fridge for up to 4 days.

MAKES 8 MUFFINS

If you are going to make some cookies, then give these a whirl. They are very simple to make, pack a lot of flavour and are named after my beautiful daughters, Chilli and Indii. We make a nut-free version so the kids can take them to school but by all means add some macadamias or your favourite nuts. If you have any type of autoimmune disease, problems with insulin or want to lose weight, it's best to avoid these cookies.

CHINDII COOKIES

3 tablespoons coconut flour

90 g (1 cup) desiccated coconut

160 g (1 cup) macadamia nuts

40 g (½ cup) quinoa* flakes or coconut flakes

60 g (½ cup) sultanas or raisins (or any dried fruit) (optional)

2 teaspoons bicarbonate of soda

pinch of Himalayan salt

155 g (1 cup) sesame seeds

100 ml coconut oil

100 ml maple syrup

4 tablespoons honey

1 teaspoon natural vanilla extract

2 eggs, lightly whisked

* See Glossary

Preheat the oven to 140°C. Line a large baking tray with baking paper.

Combine the coconut flour, desiccated coconut, macadamias, quinoa or coconut flakes, sultanas or raisins, bicarbonate of soda and salt in a food processor and pulse a few times until a chunky paste forms. Transfer the coconut flour mixture into a bowl, mix in the sesame seeds and set aside.

Melt the coconut oil in a saucepan over low heat, stir in the maple syrup, honey and vanilla and bring to a simmer. Remove from the heat and set aside.

Add the eggs to the coconut flour mixture and stir to combine. Pour in the coconut oil mixture and stir well until you have a soft, sticky dough. Shape the dough into 20 walnut-sized balls and use your hand to press them flat on the prepared tray, allowing space for the cookies to spread. Bake for 30–40 minutes, or until golden. Transfer to a wire rack to cool before eating. Store in an airtight container for up to 1 week.

MAKES 20 COOKIES

TIP

If the cookie dough seems too wet, just add some more desiccated coconut or some chia seeds; and if it's too dry, add some more coconut oil and a little water.

Lamingtons are an Australian invention, and it seems we are mighty proud of them. There are lamington-judging competitions held all around the country. (I wouldn't want to be a judge in that competition – I don't think I would make it out alive!) I wanted to include recipes in this book that people could relate to, and offer alternative and healthier ways of making them. A lamington is a square of sponge cake coated in chocolate and covered in desiccated coconut. It is completely up to you whether you decide to fill yours with jam, as I have here.

LAMINGTONS

SPONGE CAKE

200 ml coconut oil, melted

160 g (½ cup) honey

2 vanilla pods, split and seeds scraped

8 eggs

125 g (1 cup) tapioca flour*

180 g (1¾ cups) almond meal

2 teaspoons baking powder

RASPBERRY JAM

375 g (3 cups) frozen raspberries, thawed

350 g (1 cup) honey

juice of 1 lemon

CHOCOLATE-COCONUT ICING

185 ml (¾ cup) coconut oil, melted

60 g (½ cup) cacao powder

60 g (½ cup) carob powder

1 vanilla pod, split and seeds scraped

125 ml (½ cup) coconut milk

4 tablespoons honey

TO COAT

120 g (2 cups) shredded coconut

Preheat the oven to 160°C. Grease a 20 cm × 30 cm Swiss roll tin with a little melted coconut oil and line the base and sides with baking paper.

To make the sponge cake, place the coconut oil, honey and vanilla seeds in a bowl and whisk thoroughly. Set aside.

Using an electric mixer, beat the eggs for 5 minutes until thick and foamy. Gradually beat in the coconut oil mixture. Fold in the tapioca flour, almond meal and baking powder. Pour the mixture into the prepared tin and bake for 25 minutes, or until a skewer inserted in the centre comes out clean. Turn the cake out onto a wire rack to cool completely. Trim the edges and the top to form an even sheet. Cut in half horizontally, so you have two equal layers. Set aside.

To make the raspberry jam, combine the raspberries, honey and lemon juice in a small saucepan and bring to the boil over medium heat. Reduce the heat to low and simmer, stirring occasionally, for 20–30 minutes, or until the jam is thick. Remove from the heat and pass half of the jam through a fine sieve (this ensures the jam does not have a gritty texture). Mix the sieved jam back into the jam and allow to cool. Pour into a 500 ml sterilised jar (see Tip on page 245 for sterilising instructions). Refrigerate until needed.

To assemble the lamingtons, thinly spread about 3 tablespoons of raspberry jam on one side of a sponge layer. Sandwich the other sponge layer on top and cut into 5 cm squares with a long, serrated knife, then set aside.

To make the chocolate–coconut icing, combine the coconut oil, cacao, carob, vanilla seeds, coconut milk and honey in a bowl. Beat using an electric mixer on a low setting for 1 minute, or until smooth. Place the shredded coconut on a plate. Dip the sponge squares in the icing. Using two forks, gently toss the squares in the shredded coconut until evenly coated. Set aside on a wire rack for 1 hour before serving. Store leftover raspberry jam in the fridge for up to 3 months.

MAKES 24 SMALL LAMINGTONS

This is the perfect Valentine's Day dessert. I wouldn't recommend it for kids because cacao is a stimulant, but you can substitute carob instead. These are quite sweet, so please go easy.

RED VELVET CUPCAKES

80 g (½ cup) coconut flour

60 g (½ cup) arrowroot*

3 tablespoons cacao powder

1 teaspoon bicarbonate of soda

¼ teaspoon sea salt

4 eggs, separated

3 tablespoons coconut sugar*

125 ml (½ cup) coconut oil, melted

3 tablespoons honey

125 ml (½ cup) coconut milk

½ teaspoon vanilla powder

½ teaspoon apple cider vinegar

3 tablespoons beetroot juice

Whipped Coconut Cream (page 277)

raspberries, to decorate

* See Glossary

Preheat the oven to 160°C. Line an 8-hole muffin tin with paper cases.

Sift together the coconut flour, arrowroot, cacao powder, bicarbonate of soda and salt.

Combine the eggwhites and coconut sugar in a large bowl and whisk until thick and glossy.

In another bowl, combine the egg yolks, coconut oil, honey, coconut milk, vanilla, vinegar and beetroot juice and mix well. Add the dry ingredients and mix until combined. Fold in a heaped spoonful of the eggwhite to loosen, then gently fold in the rest of the eggwhite.

Pour the mixture into the paper cases until three-quarters full, then bake in the oven for 25 minutes, or until a skewer inserted in the centre of a cupcake comes out clean. Remove from the oven and allow to cool completely before removing from the tin.

Pipe the coconut cream onto the cooled cupcakes, then decorate with the raspberries.

MAKES 8 CUPCAKES

These will be sure-fire winners at your next birthday party and can be made a day or two beforehand. I've made these without added sweeteners, just the water from a young coconut, but you can add some honey or coconut nectar if you prefer. Your best bet is to use fresh young coconuts that you open yourself (see page 258 for some tips on opening young coconuts). You can use packaged coconut water but look for one that hasn't had any nasties added. If you are adventurous, you can also make savoury versions of these jellies. Try using slow-cooked meat or cooked prawns with tarragon in a fish stock. You'll need six small bowls, cups or jelly moulds for this recipe.

COCONUT JELLY WITH BERRIES

500 ml (2 cups) coconut water

1 tablespoon powdered gelatine

coconut nectar or honey, to taste (optional)

240 g mixed berries (such as raspberries, blueberries, strawberries and blackberries), plus extra for serving

flesh of 1 young coconut* (about 120 g), chopped

1 tablespoon chia seeds*

* See Glossary

Place 3 tablespoons of the coconut water in a small saucepan and sprinkle over the gelatine. Allow to soak for 2 minutes. Place the pan over medium heat and, stirring gently, bring to a simmer and heat until the gelatine has completely dissolved. Remove from the heat and set aside.

In a bowl, whisk the remaining coconut water with the coconut nectar or honey, if using. Stir in the gelatine mixture, then pour the jelly mixture into six 125 ml cups or jelly moulds until three-quarters full. Add some berries and coconut flesh and sprinkle on some chia seeds. Chill the jellies for 4 hours, or until set.

Remove the jellies from the moulds by placing the moulds in a bath of hot water for a few seconds (be careful not to submerge in the water), then turn out onto serving plates. Serve with a scattering of fresh berries.

SERVES 6

I love these little watermelon cakes on a hot summer's day when I feel like something refreshing. Even though they are not really 'cakes', I do love the play on the idea of a layered cake and the kids will get a kick out of making them. You can flavour them with whatever you like, and simply freeze the leftover watermelon pieces to use in the watermelon juice on page 259. I have added whipped coconut cream and some pistachios to give the cakes a great texture.

WATERMELON 'CAKES' WITH COCONUT CREAM AND POACHED FIGS

100 g Coconut Yoghurt (page 16)

200 g Whipped Coconut Cream (page 277)

¼ seedless watermelon (about 1.5 kg), rind removed, cut into 2 cm thick slices

30 g (¼ cup) unsalted pistachio nuts (activated if possible, see page 200), chopped

POACHED FIGS

2 tablespoons rosewater

1 tablespoon honey

2 cardamom pods, crushed

7 dried baby figs, halved

To make the poached figs, combine 150 ml of water with the rosewater, honey and cardamom pods in a small saucepan and bring to the boil over medium–high heat. Add the figs, remove from the heat, cover and set aside to cool completely.

Meanwhile, fold the coconut yoghurt and coconut cream together in a bowl until blended. Cover and refrigerate for 30 minutes to set.

Cut the watermelon into discs with a 6 cm round cookie cutter.

Place half the watermelon rounds on serving plates or a platter. Spread 1 teaspoon of the yoghurt cream on each round. Top each with one of the remaining watermelon rounds and dollop 1 tablespoon of yoghurt cream on top. Garnish the watermelon cakes with the pistachios and poached figs and drizzle on a little rosewater syrup. Serve immediately.

MAKES 7 'CAKES'

I have never had as much positive feedback for one recipe as I have had for the dairy-free 'cheesecake' in *Healthy Every Day* (well, except maybe for the cauliflower fried rice). So, I felt compelled to include another cheesecake to tantalise your tastebuds. I have to thank Cat from WildRaw in Western Australia once again for the inspiration for this recipe. You'll need to start this recipe the day before.

RASPBERRY MOUSSE CHEESECAKE

450 g macadamia nuts

300 g raspberries

125 ml (½ cup) lime juice

1 teaspoon sea salt

240 g (⅔ cup) honey

1 vanilla pod, split and seeds scraped

250 ml (1 cup) coconut oil, melted

mint leaves and raspberries, to decorate

BASE

160 g almonds (activated if possible, see page 200)

90 g (1 cup) desiccated coconut

6 medjool dates, pitted

pinch of sea salt

1½ tablespoons coconut oil, melted

Soak the macadamia nuts overnight and give them a good rinse the next morning.

Grease the base and sides of a 20 cm springform cake tin and line with baking paper.

To make the base, process the almonds and coconut in a food processor until you have a nice crumb consistency. Add the dates, salt and coconut oil and pulse until your mixture just comes together.

Press the base mixture firmly and evenly into the base of the prepared tin. Refrigerate for 1 hour, or until firm.

Blend the raspberries in the food processor until smooth. Pass the puree through a fine sieve and discard the seeds. Set aside.

Combine the macadamias, lime juice, salt, honey and vanilla seeds in the food processor and process until smooth and creamy. Add the coconut oil and process until combined.

Divide the macadamia mixture between two bowls. Pour the raspberry puree into one of the bowls and mix until well combined.

Pour the plain mixture over the base and tap the tin gently on the bench to remove any air bubbles. Next pour in the raspberry mixture and gently tap the tin again. Place in the freezer for 4 hours, or until firm.

To serve, remove the cheesecake from the tin while frozen and transfer to a serving platter. Place in the fridge for 2–4 hours to completely thaw. Decorate with mint leaves and raspberries and serve.

The cheesecake can be stored in an airtight container in the fridge for 1–2 weeks or in the freezer for 3 months.

SERVES 8–10

I couldn't write a family-friendly cookbook without including a birthday cake, could I? This epic cake will take a bit of time and effort, but I promise it will be worth it. And when you bring it out at your next kids' party, no-one will guess that it is dairy, grain and refined sugar free – until you tell them, that is! There are a number of different elements, so I suggest preparing them in the order they are listed in the method below – this way, by the time your almond sponges have cooled, you'll have all of the other elements ready to assemble the cake.

BIRTHDAY CAKE WITH COCONUT ICING

PASTRY CREAM

600 ml coconut cream

1 vanilla pod, split and seeds scraped

6 egg yolks

90 g (¼ cup) honey

1½ tablespoons powdered gelatine, soaked in 4 tablespoons extra coconut milk

PISTACHIO PASTE

250 g (2 cups) unsalted, raw, shelled pistachios

80 g (⅓ cup) coconut sugar

125 ml (½ cup) macadamia oil

Ingredient list continued over page

PASTRY CREAM

To make the pastry cream, place the coconut cream, vanilla seeds and pod in a saucepan and bring to a light boil over medium heat, stirring occasionally. Strain through a sieve and discard the vanilla pod. Whisk the egg yolks and honey together until thick and pale. Add the coconut cream a little at a time, whisking constantly until smooth. Return the mixture to the saucepan, place over medium–low heat, stirring constantly with a spatula for 4–8 minutes, until the custard thickens and coats the spatula. Remove from the heat and whisk in the gelatine mixture until well incorporated. Pour into a bowl and place plastic wrap directly onto the pastry cream to prevent a skin from forming. Refrigerate for 2 hours, or until set.

PISTACHIO PASTE

Preheat the oven to 150°C. Line a baking tray with baking paper. Scatter the pistachios in a single layer on the tray and roast in the oven for 10 minutes, or until golden. Leave to cool. Place the coconut sugar and 3 tablespoons of water in a saucepan over medium heat. Bring to the boil and let it bubble away until it reaches 121°C on a sugar thermometer. Add the pistachios and mix well. Pour the crystalised pistachios onto the lined baking tray. Spread them out into a single layer and leave for an 1–2 hours to cool completely. Break the pistachio praline into pieces and process in a food processor to fine crumbs. Add the macadamia oil and continue to process for 5 minutes, or until a fine, thick paste forms. Add a little more more oil if necessary. Refrigerate until ready to use.

Recipe continued over page

WHITE CHOCOLATE DECORATIONS

130 g cocoa butter

2 tablespoons coconut milk powder

2 teaspoons maple syrup

pinch of fine sea salt

½–1 teaspoon natural food colouring (such as beetroot powder, turmeric powder, chlorophyll, blueberry juice or raspberry juice)

ALMOND SPONGE

360 g (about 12) eggwhites

300 g honey

12 eggs

390 g (4 cups) almond meal

80 g (½ cup) coconut flour

1½ tablespoons baking powder

180 g (1½ cups) arrowroot*

160 ml coconut oil, melted

125 ml (½ cup) maple syrup

9 strawberries, hulled and thinly sliced

SPICE SYRUP

90 g (¼ cup) honey

1 vanilla pod, split and seeds scraped

2 cinnamon sticks

COCONUT ICING

650 ml coconut oil, chilled

260 g (¾ cup) honey

2 teaspoons coconut cream

* See Glossary

WHITE CHOCOLATE DECORATIONS

To make the white chocolate decorations, line a baking tray with baking paper. Place the cocoa butter in a heatproof bowl over a saucepan of just-simmering water. Do not allow the bowl to come into contact with the water otherwise the chocolate might overheat. Stir with a metal spoon until the cocoa butter is smooth and melted. Remove from the heat and whisk in the coconut milk powder, maple syrup and salt. Add the food colouring and mix until shiny and smooth. Place the bowl of chocolate over a bowl of iced water, again making sure the bowl with the chocolate doesn't comes into contact with the water. Stir gently until the chocolate thickens and coats the back of the spoon (about 26–28°C, if you have a sugar thermometer). Spread the chocolate onto the baking tray and place in the fridge for 30 minutes, or until set. Allow the chocolate sit at room temperature for 10 minutes before cutting out your desired shapes using a cookie cutter. Pop the chocolate shapes back in the fridge until you are ready to decorate.

ALMOND SPONGE

Preheat the oven to 160°C. Grease two 20 cm round cake tins and line the bases with baking paper.

Beat the eggwhites and honey in a large bowl with an electric mixer until the mixture forms soft peaks. Add the whole eggs and continue to mix for a further 2 minutes, or until the mixture has doubled in size.

Gently fold in the almond meal, coconut flour, baking powder and arrowroot, then stir through the coconut oil. Divide the mixture evenly between the prepared tins, levelling the tops with a palette knife.

Bake for 15 minutes, or until lightly golden. Cover with foil and cook for a further 30 minutes, or until a skewer inserted into each cake comes out clean. Leave to cool in the tins.

SPICE SYRUP

To make the spice syrup, place all the ingredients and 150 ml of water in a small saucepan and bring to the boil over medium heat. Remove from the heat and allow to cool before using.

COCONUT ICING

To make the coconut icing, process all the ingredients in a food processor until smooth. Transfer to a bowl, cover and set aside until ready to use.

TO ASSEMBLE

Before you turn the cakes out of their tins, check that they have level tops. If they are domed, slice off some of the top until flat. Carefully turn the cakes out onto wire racks and check that they are the same height, slicing off a little more of the top until they are of equal height. Next, carefully cut each cake in half horizontally, so that you now have 4 round, flat discs of equal thickness.

Place one cake onto a large plate. Brush the top with the spice syrup, then evenly spread 3 tablespoons of the pistachio paste on top. Fill a piping bag with the coconut icing and pipe a circle border around the top of the cake. This will prevent the filling from oozing out the sides.

Fill another piping bag with the pastry cream and pipe it into the centre of the cake. Spread out the pastry cream with a palette knife until it reaches the coconut icing border. Top with a layer of sliced strawberries. Carefully place the second cake round on top, then place in the freezer for 30 minutes to set.

Repeat this procedure with the third cake round, layering with the spice syrup, pistachio paste, coconut icing, pastry cream and strawberries, leaving the top of the last cake round bare. Freeze for 2 hours.

To ice the cake, place 6 tablespoons of coconut icing on top of the cake. With a long palette knife, spread the icing over the top and sides to form a thin, smooth layer. You can dip the palette knife in some hot water occasionally to help make the icing as smooth as possible. Place the cake in the fridge and chill for 20 minutes.

When the first layer of icing has set, place half of the remaining icing on top of the cake. Again, spread the icing out on the top and sides of the cake until smooth. (This double layer of icing creates a smoother finish, as the first layer seals the crumbs from the cake and prevents them from spreading on the second layer.)

Return the cake to the fridge for 20 minutes. Place some of the remaining icing in a piping bag with a small tip. Pipe a small amount of the icing onto the back of the white chocolate shapes, then stick them onto the cake. Return the cake to the fridge until ready to serve.

SERVES 10

I was recently filming with a producer mate of mine who was all for the paleo diet, except for one small issue: he didn't want to give up ice cream. 'Mate,' I said, 'I have just the thing for you.' This paleo ice cream will put a smile on your face – and make you feel like you are not missing out. More importantly, you can eat this knowing that it is a lot better for your system than the dairy and refined-sugar version that you have been gobbling down for years. Please feel free to adapt this recipe and flavour it with whichever spices you love: cinnamon, cardamom, saffron, ginger, licorice. Herbs such as mint and basil work really well, too.

BLUEBERRY AND CHIA ICE CREAM

450 ml coconut cream

450 ml coconut milk

4 egg yolks

180 g (½ cup) honey or maple syrup

3 tablespoons black or white chia seeds*

BLUEBERRY JAM

600 g frozen blueberries, thawed

240 g (⅔ cup) honey

juice of 1 lemon

* See Glossary

To make the blueberry jam, combine all the ingredients in a small saucepan, mix well and place over medium heat. Bring to the boil, then reduce the heat to low and simmer, stirring occasionally, for 35–40 minutes, or until the jam is thick.

Remove from the heat and set aside to cool. Pour the jam into a 750 ml sterilised jar (see below for instructions), seal and refrigerate until required.

To make the ice cream, place the coconut cream and coconut milk in a saucepan and bring to the boil, stirring occasionally. Remove from the heat.

In a large heatproof bowl, whisk the egg yolks and honey or maple syrup until light and fluffy.

Pour half of the hot coconut cream mixture into the egg mixture and whisk well. Whisk in the remaining hot coconut cream mixture, then pour into a clean saucepan. Cook over medium heat, stirring with a wooden spoon or spatula, until the mixture thickens slightly to form a custard and coats the back of the spoon. Strain through a fine sieve into a bowl. Cover with plastic wrap and chill for at least 2 hours.

Pour the coconut custard into an ice cream maker and churn according to the manufacturer's instructions. Fold in 300 g of the blueberry jam and the chia seeds, transfer to an airtight container and freeze until firm.

Place the ice cream in the refrigerator to soften a little before serving. The leftover jam can be stored in the refrigerator for up to 3 months.

MAKES 1.3 LITRES

> TIP

To sterilise your jam jars, wash them in hot, soapy water and run them through a hot rinse cycle in your dishwasher. (If you don't have a dishwasher, boil the jars and lids in a large pot on the stove for 10 minutes, then place them on a tray in a 150°C oven for 10 minutes, or until dry.)

These are wonderful fun to make for Easter and so healthy compared to the store-bought versions. Show your kids the four or five ingredients that go into these eggs; then show them what is on the label of most manufactured Easter eggs and explain the difference. You will need a candy thermometer, egg or bunny moulds and sheets of coloured foil for this recipe. They can all be purchased online or at specialty cake decorating and chocolate supply stores.

EASTER EGGS AND BUNNIES

| 250 g cocoa butter |
| 120 g cacao powder or carob powder |
| 100 g honey |
| 3½ tablespoons coconut oil |
| 3–5 drops mint oil or orange oil (optional) |

NOTES

We used a twin-mould 9.5 cm 3D Easter egg chocolate tray, six-mould mini bunny chocolate tray and 23 cm sheet of coloured foil for this recipe, but feel free to use whichever size and shape moulds you like.

The process of stirring the chocolate as it cools is called tempering and ensures the chocolate will be smooth and shiny with a pleasant flavour and that the honey will not separate once set.

Place the cocoa butter in a heatproof bowl over a saucepan of just-simmering water. Do not allow the bowl to come into contact with the water. Stir the cocoa butter with a metal spoon until it is smooth and melted and reaches a maximum temperature of 45°C. Remove from the heat and whisk in the cacao or carob powder, honey and coconut oil. Add the mint or orange oil (if using) and mix until shiny and smooth.

Place the bowl of chocolate over a bowl of iced water, making sure the chocolate does not touch the water. Stir until the chocolate thickens and coats the back of the spoon. Once it has cooled to 25–28°C, remove the bowl from the iced water. You may need to do this in batches if you find that solid lumps are forming. If this occurs, remove the bowl from the iced water and keep mixing until the chocolate has melted evenly.

Pipe or spoon the chocolate into the moulds. Swirl the chocolate around until each mould is completely coated, using a pastry brush if necessary, and remove any excess chocolate from the flat surface of the moulds. Tap the moulds on the workbench to remove any air bubbles. Using the flat side of a knife, carefully scrape and smooth the top edges of the moulds. (Levelling the edges is essential so that the two halves adhere, properly.) If the chocolate starts to set in the bowl while you are filling the moulds, melt it down to 25–28°C again. Transfer the moulds to the fridge for 15 minutes. Repeat this process two or three times until a thick layer of chocolate lines each mould. Place in the fridge for 30 minutes, or until set.

Preheat the oven to 50°C. Warm a baking tray in the oven for 8 minutes. Remove the moulds from the fridge and carefully turn out the chocolate by flipping the moulds over and gently tapping. Place on a clean work surface, taking care not to handle the chocolate too much, as it will start to melt. Place the open edges of each chocolate half directly on the warmed tray for a few seconds, then join together, pushing gently to seal. Repeat until all the chocolates are sealed. Wrap in coloured foil and store in the fridge.

MAKES 2 EGGS OR 6 MINI BUNNIES

I can still remember the instantly refreshing feeling you get from sucking on an ice-cold popsicle on a hot summer's day, so I just had to include a recipe that you and your kids can easily make at home. They take no time at all to prepare, but they do take about 6 hours to freeze, so it's best to make them the night before, otherwise you'll have hungry munchkins hanging around the kitchen hankering for the pops to freeze. Some of my favourite fruits to use are antioxidant-rich berries, refreshing watermelon and mangoes with a squeeze of lime juice.

FRUIT SALAD POPSICLES

2 young coconuts*

selection of fruit of your choice (such as strawberries, grapes, mangoes, lychees, kiwi fruit, raspberries, pineapple)

* See Glossary

Open the coconuts by cutting a circular hole in the top of each one. Strain the coconut water and set aside.

Cut the fruit into bite-sized pieces (not too small – you want to enjoy the lovely texture of frozen fruit). Arrange the fruit in eight 80 ml popsicle moulds, making sure the pieces fit very snugly. Pour enough coconut water into each mould to just cover the fruit. Insert a popsicle stick in the middle of each mould and freeze until solid, about 6 hours.

MAKES 8

I already know what you are thinking: next birthday party the kids are definitely going to be eating these – unless, of course, the party happens to be mid-winter. Anyway, these snow cones are a sure-fire winner and a thirst-quencher anytime. They are so easy to make and are as pure as the driven snow! Just make sure your coconut water has no added sugar or other nasties.

BERRY SNOW CONES

400 g fresh or frozen (thawed) mixed berries of your choice (such as blueberries, raspberries, strawberries, cranberries and blackberries)

juice of ½ orange

1 tablespoon honey, or to taste

200 ml coconut water

ice cubes

Place the berries, orange juice, honey and coconut water in a bender and blend until smooth. Pass the puree through a fine sieve and discard the seeds. Set aside.

Place the ice cubes in a food processor and process until fine.

Scoop the crushed ice into cone cups, pour over some berry puree and serve immediately.

SERVES 4

DRINKS

Macadamias are my go-to nut. They are full of good fats and essential minerals and are native to Australia. They are the one Australian native species grown on a large scale for food, but I can see more native foods emerging in the mainstream market over the coming years. Australian native food is so healthy it eclipses most other food. In the 1920s, dentist and widely respected Canadian nutrition researcher Weston A. Price studied the diet and lifestyles of the world's native peoples and concluded that the diet and lifestyle of the Australian Aborigine was the healthiest. It is my goal and vision to bring more of that traditional diet back to everyone living in Australia, and we can start with macadamias, then move onto quandongs, wattle seeds, kakadu plums . . .

MACADAMIA AND BANANA SMOOTHIE

1 large banana, frozen

¼ vanilla pod, split and seeds scraped, or a pinch of vanilla powder

pinch of ground cinnamon, plus extra to serve

5 macadamia nuts (activated if possible, see page 200)

185 ml (¾ cup) almond milk (to make your own, see page 258)

2 teaspoons flaxseed meal* (optional)

1 tablespoon honey or to taste (optional)

* See Glossary

Place all the ingredients in a blender and blend until smooth. Pour into a glass, dust with an extra pinch of cinnamon and serve immediately.

SERVES 1

Kefir is a great source of vitamins, minerals, probiotics and a variety of other unique compounds that can greatly contribute to your overall health and wellbeing. Kefir was traditionally made using raw milk that was then fermented; however, I much prefer using either coconut milk or coconut water. Try experimenting with different fruits and herbs for added flavour and medicinal qualities.

YOUNG COCONUT KEFIR

3–4 fresh young coconuts*

1 packet vegetable starter culture* (this will weigh 2–5 g, depending on the brand)

* See Glossary

TIPS

It is important that all materials that come into contact with the kefir are sterilised. You want to grow good bacteria, not the bad stuff, so boil or wash everything in very hot water. Also make sure you wash your hands well before starting.

Glass jars and storage bottles are preferable to plastic since kefir actually breaks down plastic and you may end up eating it. Limited contact is fine, but prolonged contact is discouraged.

It is very important that you use coconut water from fresh young coconuts. Store-bought varieties do not work as they are pasteurised.

You will need a 1.5 litre preserving jar or bottle with an airlock lid for this recipe. Wash the jar, a small saucepan and a spoon in hot soapy water, then sterilise them by running them through a hot rinse cycle on your dishwasher.

Open the coconuts by cutting a circular hole in the tops. Strain the coconut water into the sterilised saucepan, place over low heat and bring to 31–32°C. Use a candy thermometer to check the temperature or wash your hands very well and dip in your finger. At 32°C, it will feel lukewarm, just below body temperature. Be careful not to heat it above 37°C, as the microflora and many of the enzymes and vitamins will be destroyed.

Pour the coconut water into the sterilised jar, then add the starter culture and stir with the sterilised spoon until dissolved. Close the lid and put in a dark place to ferment at 21–24°C for 36–48 hours (an esky is good). Your kefir is ready when the water turns from relatively clear to cloudy white. Taste test it after 36 hours by pouring some into a glass. It should taste tart and tangy, like champagne. If it still tastes sweet, leave it for a little longer. Once ready, it will last for up to 2 weeks in the fridge.

MAKES ABOUT 1.5 LITRES

VARIATIONS

Strawberry and mint kefir
Wash and halve eight strawberries, then add them to the finished fermented kefir with a small handful of mint leaves. Close the lid, place in a dark spot and leave to ferment at 21–24°C for a further 24 hours. Pour into a sterilised glass jug with a lid and refrigerate. Strain and discard the fruit pulp before drinking.

Raspberry, clove and ginger kefir
Add 60 g raspberries, six cloves and 1 tablespoon finely grated ginger to the finished fermented kefir. Close the lid and place in a dark spot to ferment at 21–24°C for a further 24 hours. Pour into a sterilised glass jug with a lid and refrigerate. Strain before drinking.

Raspberry, clove and ginger kefir

Strawberry and mint kefir

NUT MILK

1 cup activated nuts (such as almonds, macadamias, hazelnuts or walnuts) (page 200)

Place the nuts in a blender with 1 litre of water and blend for a couple of minutes until smooth.

Line a large bowl with a piece of muslin large enough to allow the muslin to hang over the edge of the bowl. Pour the blended nuts and water into the bowl. Pick up the corners of the muslin, bring together and squeeze out all the nut milk. (The leftover solids can be used to make bliss balls or in baking recipes in place of almond meal.)

Pour the nut milk into a 1 litre glass jar or bottle, cover, place in the fridge and give it a good shake when you want to use it. The nut milk will last for 3–4 days in the fridge.

MAKES 1 LITRE

HIBISCUS ICED TEA

½ cup jamaica (dried hibiscus)*

155 g (1 cup) fresh or frozen blueberries, plus extra to serve

1–2 tablespoons lime juice

honey, to taste

ice cubes, to serve

* See Glossary

Place the jamaica in a large stain-proof container, such as a teapot, and pour on 1 litre of boiling water. Allow to steep for 15 minutes.

While the tea is steeping, place the blueberries, 750 ml of water and 1 tablespoon lime juice in a blender. Blend on high speed until the liquid is as smooth as possible. Pour through a fine strainer into a jug.

Strain the steeped tea into the blueberry mixture. Stir, taste and, if needed, add more lime juice and sweeten to taste with honey.

Chill. Stir and serve with ice and a few whole blueberries.

SERVES 6

COCONUT WATER WITH GINGER, MANGO AND MINT

1 litre (4 cups) coconut water

1 mango, cut into 2 cm cubes

6 cm piece of ginger, peeled and julienned

1 handful of mint leaves

ice cubes (optional)

Place the coconut water, mango, ginger and mint in a glass jug, cover and refrigerate for a few hours to infuse. For best results, leave overnight and store in the fridge so the fruit stays nice and fresh. Serve with ice if you wish. This will last for 3–4 days in the fridge.

MAKES 1 LITRE

WATERMELON JUICE WITH CHIA AND BERRIES

500 g watermelon, peeled and cut into pieces

½ Lebanese cucumber

½ lime, peeled

100 ml coconut water

ice cubes

60 g blueberries

1 teaspoon chia seeds

mint leaves

Juice the watermelon, cucumber and lime in a juicer. Pour the coconut water through the juicer to mix in with the juice.

Pour the juice into glasses, add the ice cubes and finish with the blueberries, a sprinkle of chia seeds and mint leaves.

SERVES 2

Kombucha is made by fermenting sweet tea. It helps with digestion and strengthens your immune system. The tea is cultured with a scoby, which is a colony of bacteria and yeasts. Scobies are usually created by feeding and growing these particular sets of bacteria; as they grow they are then divided and shared with others. If you don't know anyone who can give you a scoby, you can purchase them through specialist fermenters, such as Kitsa's Kitchen. You can also create your own scoby from a bottle of kombucha bought from a health food store. You can use black, green, oolong or white tea as a base for your kombucha, and by adding sugar you create an energy source for the scoby. The sugar is eaten up by the bacteria so there is very little left in the final product.

KOMBUCHA

250 g (1 cup) coconut sugar*, honey or molasses

5 teaspoons organic loose-leaf black tea

250 ml (1 cup) finished kombucha liquid (from a previous batch, a store-bought bottle, or from the liquid the scoby comes in)

1 kombucha scoby

* See Glossary

TIP

You will need four 1 litre sterilised glass bottles to store your finished kombucha. To sterilise the bottles, wash them in very hot, soapy water and run them through a hot rinse cycle in your dishwasher. If you don't have a dishwasher, boil the bottles in a large pot on the stove for 10 minutes, then place on a tray in a 150°C oven for 10 minutes, or until dry.

Bring 750 ml of filtered water to the boil in a stainless steel saucepan. Add the coconut sugar or other sweetener and stir until dissolved. Remove from the heat and add the loose-leaf tea. Allow to cool.

Pour the sweet tea through a fine plastic strainer into a 3.5-litre glass jar with a wide mouth (don't use metal or plastic as these materials can damage the cultures in the scoby). Add the finished kombucha liquid and scoby to the jar, along with 2.45 litres of filtered water. Cover the top of your jar with cheesecloth and secure it with a rubber band. Leave undisturbed for 1–3 weeks in a warm, dark place – you are aiming for 18–28°C. On top of the fridge works well or, if you live in a colder climate, you can use a heating mat like those used for seedlings. As your kombucha ferments, a new scoby will grow attached to the original one to the width of your container.

After a week of fermenting, taste your kombucha to determine if it's ready to drink. It should be moderately fizzy and have a sweet and sour flavor, with a slight hint of tea. If the mixture still tastes too sweet, leave it to ferment for a few more days. If you're happy with the taste, use clean hands to remove the scoby and separate it from the new one. You will now have two scobies, which you can use to make more kombucha (or you can give one to a friend who is interested in making their own). If you don't want to make another batch of kombucha straight away, you can store the scobies in a solution of sweetened tea on the bench. Don't put the scobies in the fridge or they will go into hibernation.

Transfer the kombucha to sterilised glass bottles for storage, leaving about 1.5 cm at the top. Allow the bottled kombucha to sit at room temperature for a day or two to ferment a bit more and to build up carbonation, then refrigerate until ready to drink. The kombucha will last in the fridge for up to three months, but it's better to drink it sooner rather than later.

MAKES 4 LITRES

Beet kvass is an unusual and delicious drink that I absolutely love. It is touted as a great liver cleanser and is widely used in Europe as part of natural approach to chronic fatigue, allergies and digestive disorders. Kvass is pretty simple to make, though you may want to wear disposable gloves – unless you don't mind having purple hands for a few days. Try to get your kids to have some of this in small quantities – it's a great alternative to red cordial and you can also freeze the mixture into ice blocks or popsicles as a refreshing summer treat.

BEET KVASS

2–4 beetroot

1 tablespoon sea salt or Himalayan salt

½ sachet vegetable starter culture* or 3 tablespoons sauerkraut brine (to make your own kraut, see page 178)

* See Glossary

You will need a sterilised 1.5 litre preserving jar with an airlock lid for this recipe. You will also need to sterilise the knife, chopping board, glass measuring jug and stainless steel spoon you will be using. To do this, wash the jar and utensils in very hot, soapy water. Dry well and set aside. Alternatively, run them through a hot rinse cycle in the dishwasher.

Wash and scrub the beetroot (peel them if they are not organic). Chop the beetroot into 1.5 cm cubes and place in the jar.

Mix the salt, 250 ml of filtered water and the starter culture or sauerkraut brine in a glass measuring jug, then pour into the jar.

Fill the jar with filtered water, leaving 2 cm free at the top. Cover the jar with the lid and a piece of muslin secured with an elastic band. Leave on the kitchen counter at room temperature for 3–5 days to ferment. Chill before drinking. The kvass will keep for 2 weeks in the fridge once opened.

MAKES 1.5 LITRES

> **TIP**

If you don't want to use sauerkraut juice or starter culture, you can double the amount of salt, though this will take longer to ferment.

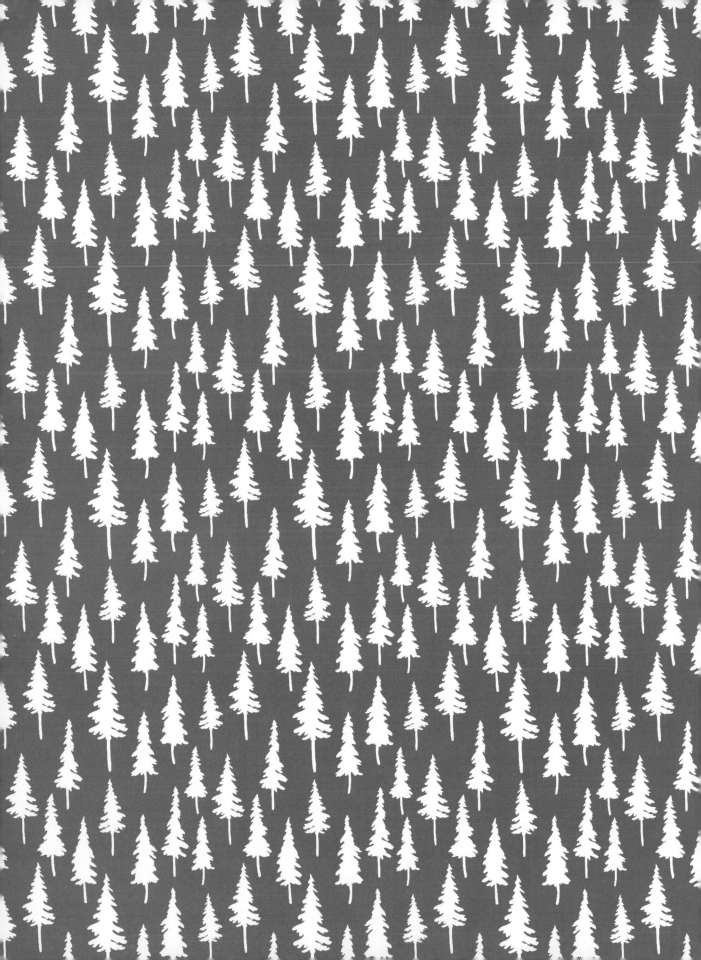

CHRISTMAS

Christmas ham is one tradition that I am happy to continue in our household as not only is it super easy and delicious, but there are leftovers for days, if not weeks. Having quality protein in the fridge is one of the most important pieces of advice I can give to anyone moving to a paleo diet as it helps you to feel fuller for longer. If you are looking for ideas for your leftover ham, you can eat it with green eggs for breakfast (thanks Dr Seuss), shave it through a gorgeous summer salad or even serve it with some Christmas Kraut (page 272).

GLAZED CHRISTMAS HAM

1 × 5 kg cooked, cold leg of ham

3 large apples of your choice, halved

3 peaches, halved and stoned

GLAZE

260 g (¾ cup) honey

zest and juice of 1 orange

1½ teaspoons ground yellow mustard seeds

1½ teaspoons ground cinnamon

¼ teaspoon ground cloves

¼ teaspoon freshly grated nutmeg

¼ teaspoon ground allspice

Preheat the oven to 160°C.

Prepare the ham by lifting off the skin but leaving the fat. Score a diamond pattern into the fat. (This helps to open the ham up and to allow the flavour to penetrate into the meat.)

To make the glaze, combine all the ingredients with 3 tablespoons of water in a bowl and mix well.

Spread the glaze over the ham. Place the ham in a roasting tin and pour in water to a depth of 2 cm. Bake for 30 minutes. Remove from the oven and scatter the apples and peaches around the ham. Return to the oven and bake for another 30–60 minutes, basting the fruit and ham from time to time. (Be careful not to let the ham burn.) Cover with foil and set aside in a warm place to rest for 15 minutes before slicing.

Slice the ham and serve with the spiced fruit.

SERVES 15–20

I am pleased to learn that some well-intentioned farmers in Australia are now producing free-range, hormone- and antibiotic-free turkeys – it is a step in the right direction. I have created a basic but delicious recipe for roast turkey here – please feel free to tweak the stuffing ingredients to your taste. You will need to start this recipe a day ahead. And if your turkey is frozen, thaw it in the fridge for approximately 3 days before you're ready to cook.

ROAST TURKEY WITH HERB MARINADE

1 × 3.5 kg turkey

good-quality fat*, melted

2 carrots, sliced lengthways

1 onion, sliced

4 garlic cloves, peeled

5 fresh bay leaves

1.25 litres (5 cups) chicken stock (to make your own, see page 86)

2 tablespoons tapioca flour*

MARINADE

2 large handfuls of mint leaves

2 large handfuls of curly parsley leaves

2 large handfuls of coriander leaves

4 garlic cloves, peeled

240 ml lemon juice

250 ml (1 cup) white wine

200 g good-quality fat*, melted

2 teaspoons ground cumin

salt and freshly ground black pepper

STUFFING

2 tablespoons good-quality fat*

1 onion, finely chopped

4 garlic confit cloves (to make your own, see page 172) or roasted garlic cloves

3 rashers of bacon, diced

4 tablespoons chopped curly parsley

3 tablespoons dukkah

450 g pork mince

1 teaspoon finely grated lemon zest

* See Glossary

To make the marinade, combine all the ingredients in a food processor and blend until smooth. Place the turkey in a large shallow dish, pat dry with paper towel and pour over the marinade, massaging it into the skin and inside the cavity. Cover with plastic wrap and refrigerate for 24 hours. Every few hours massage the marinade onto the bird.

The next day, remove the turkey from the fridge and sit for 1 hour to reach room temperature. Preheat the oven to 240°C.

To make the stuffing, heat the fat in a saucepan over medium heat. Add the onion and cook for 5 minutes, or until soft. Crush the garlic confit and add to the pan, along with the bacon. Cook until just starting to colour (3–5 minutes). Remove from the heat and set aside to cool. Add the remaining ingredients and mix until combined.

Fill the turkey cavity with the stuffing, cross the legs over and tie with kitchen string. Place in a large roasting tin and pour in any remaining excess marinade. Rub the turkey with some melted fat and season with salt and pepper. Add the carrot, onion, garlic and bay leaves, cover with foil and place in the oven. Reduce the oven to 180°C and roast for about 2 hours, basting regularly. To brown the skin, remove the foil in the final 40 minutes. The turkey is cooked once the juices run clear when the inside of the thigh is pierced with a skewer. Cooking time may vary – it should take about 40 minutes per kilogram. Transfer the turkey to a platter, cover with foil and rest for 20 minutes.

To make the gravy, place the chicken stock in a saucepan over medium heat and simmer until reduced by half (about 20 minutes). Skim the fat from the roasting tin and discard. Mix the tapioca flour with 3 tablespoons of water and add to the tin. Stir in the reduced stock and bring to the boil over medium heat, stirring occasionally. Reduce the heat to low and simmer until the sauce thickens. Strain into a jug. Carve the turkey and serve with the gravy.

SERVES 8–10

Prawns and avocado are a divine combination and it is incredibly easy to create delicious variations of this simple recipe. Start by sourcing the freshest, plumpest prawns you can get your hands on, find some gorgeous ripe avocados and then all you need to do is add your favourite dressing, marinade, sauce or mayonnaise. Finish with some herbs and maybe some nuts and seeds and you have a pretty fabulous dish. In this version, I've added preserved lemon for a unique twist on guacamole that will have your guests or family thinking you spent *hours* in the kitchen.

KING PRAWNS WITH PRESERVED LEMON GUACAMOLE

16 raw king prawns

3 tablespoons lemon-infused extra-virgin olive oil, plus extra to serve

1 tablespoon lemon juice

1 teaspoon chopped dill

sea salt and freshly ground black pepper

1 red capsicum, diced

1 handful of coriander leaves

1 handful of dill leaves

GUACAMOLE

½ red capsicum

2 avocados, sliced

1 Roma tomato, deseeded and diced

1 small red chilli, deseeded and finely chopped

¼ red onion, finely chopped

1 tablespoon finely chopped preserved lemon

1 tablespoon chopped coriander leaves

2 tablespoons lemon juice

2 tablespoons lemon-infused extra-virgin olive oil

Cook the prawns in salted boiling water for 2–3 minutes, or until pink and firm. Transfer to a bowl of iced water to cool completely. Peel and devein, keeping the tails intact.

Combine the olive oil, lemon juice and dill in a bowl and season with salt and pepper. Whisk to combine, then add the prawns and toss until well coated. Cover with plastic wrap and marinate for 5 minutes in the fridge.

Preheat the oven to 200°C.

To make the guacamole, place the capsicum, skin-side up, on a baking tray. Roast in the oven for 10–15 minutes, or until the skin blisters and blackens. Place the capsicum in a bowl, cover with plastic wrap and set aside to steam for 5 minutes. Peel and discard the skin, then chop the flesh. Combine the avocado, roast capsicum, tomato, chilli, onion, preserved lemon, coriander, lemon juice and olive oil in a bowl and gently mix. Season with salt and pepper to taste.

Spoon the guacamole onto a serving platter, top with the marinated prawns, garnish with the capsicum, coriander and dill and serve with a drizzle of extra oil.

SERVES 4

'Sour, spice and all things nice' is the way I like to describe this Christmas kraut. Cabbage and apple are pretty awesome in kraut, but when combined with cinnamon, clove and allspice and fermented for a week or two before Christmas, you have the absolute best accompaniment to serve with your Christmas ham (page 266) or roast turkey (page 268). You could even have it with your eggs when you wake up on Christmas morning. Damn, it is good!

CHRISTMAS KRAUT

1 teaspoon whole cloves

650 g red cabbage

1 green apple, cored but skin on

1½ teaspoons sea salt

1 teaspoon ground allspice

1 sachet vegetable starter culture*
(this will weigh 2–5 g, depending
on the brand)

2 cinnamon sticks

1 orange, sliced into rounds

1 radish, thinly sliced

See Glossary

TIP

Because I love fermenting veggies so much, I have created a range of jars that are purpose-made to do exactly this. If you do use one of my Culture For Life fermentation jars, there is no need to cover and weight the vegetables with a folded cabbage leaf and a shot glass, as the jar has an in-built weighting system. There is also no need to cover with a tea towel, as there is a silicone cover provided to block out the light.

You will need a 2.5 litre sterilised preserving jar with an airlock lid for this recipe. You will also need to sterilise the knife, spoon, chopping board and glass or stainless steel bowl and jug you will be using. To do this, wash the jar and utensils thoroughly in very hot water or run them through a hot rinse cycle in the dishwasher.

Place the cloves in a small piece of muslin, tie into a bundle with kitchen string and set aside. Remove the outer leaves of the cabbage. Choose one of the outer leaves, wash well and set aside. Shred the cabbage and apple in a food processor with a shredding attachment, or use a mandoline or knife to chop by hand. Transfer the cabbage and apple to a large glass or stainless steel bowl and sprinkle over the salt and allspice. Mix well, cover and set aside.

Dissolve the starter culture in water according to the packet instructions (the amount of water will depend on the brand you are using). Add to the cabbage along with the bag of cloves, cinnamon, orange and radish and gently mix. Fill the prepared jar with the cabbage mixture, pressing down well with a large spoon or potato masher to remove any air pockets. Leave 2 cm of room free at the top. The cabbage mixture should be completely submerged in the liquid, so add more water if necessary.

Fold up the reserved cabbage leaf and place it on top of the mixture, then add a small glass weight (a shot glass is ideal) to keep everything submerged. Close the lid, then wrap a tea towel around the side of the jar to block out the light. Store the jar in a dark place with a temperature of 16–23°C for 10–14 days. (You can place the jar in an esky to maintain a more consistent temperature.) The longer you leave the jar, the higher the level of good bacteria present and the tangier the flavour.

Chill before eating. Once opened, the kraut will last for up to 2 months in the fridge submerged in the liquid. If unopened, it will keep for up to 9 months in the fridge.

MAKES 1 × 2.5 LITRE JAR

I guarantee that everyone will be asking you to share this gluten-, dairy- and refined-sugar-free recipe. These mince pies make such great gifts, especially for friends or rellies with a food intolerance or allergy. You will need ten 7.5 cm flan tins and a star-shaped cookie cutter for this recipe.

MINCE PIES

SWEET PASTRY

100 g (1 cup) almond meal

100 g (¾ cup) coconut flour

60 g (½ cup) arrowroot*

210 ml coconut oil or 210 g ghee*, chilled

6 tablespoons honey or coconut sugar*

2 eggs

MINCE FILLING

100 g (¾ cup) raisins

100 g (¾ cup) sultanas

50 g (⅓ cup) dried cranberries

50 g (⅓ cup) currants

50 g (⅓ cup) golden sultanas

1 granny smith apple, peeled, cored and finely chopped

100 g (about ¼) pineapple, chopped

3 tablespoons honey

1 teaspoon ground cinnamon

½ teaspoon freshly grated nutmeg

½ teaspoon ground ginger

zest and juice of 2 oranges

* See Glossary

To make the sweet pastry, mix the almond meal, coconut flour and arrowroot in a bowl. Cut the coconut oil or ghee into small pieces and use your fingertips to work it into the almond meal mixture to form fine crumbs. Add the honey and mix until to form a dough. Transfer to a surface dusted with arrowroot and knead until smooth (the dough will be slightly sticky). Wrap the dough in plastic wrap and refrigerate for 30 minutes, or until it is firm enough to roll out. (The dough can be stored in the fridge for up to 1 week and in the freezer for up to 3 months.)

To make the mince filling, place all the ingredients in a saucepan over low heat and stir to combine. Gently simmer, stirring occasionally, for 30 minutes. (Do not boil or the mixture will burn and taste bitter.) Turn off the heat, transfer the mixture to a food processor and pulse a few times until coarsely chopped. Set aside to cool.

Preheat the oven to 160°C. Grease ten 7.5 cm flan tins.

Place the dough between two sheets of baking paper and roll out until 5 mm thick. Transfer the pastry and baking paper to a large tray and chill for 5 minutes to slightly firm. Remove the top layer of baking paper and, using a 9 cm round cutter, cut out 10 rounds. Reroll the offcuts and cut out ten 7 cm star shapes.

Line the prepared flan tins with the pastry rounds and trim to ensure you have smooth clean edges. Because this dough does not contain gluten it will feel quite different to regular dough and may crack a little more easily. If cracks do form, gently bind the dough together with your fingers to seal. Add 2 tablespoons of mince to each pastry case and level with the back of a spoon. Place a pastry star on top of each pie and transfer the pies to a baking tray. Bake for 15 minutes, or until the pastry is golden. Set aside for 5 minutes to cool before removing from the tins and transferring to a wire rack to cool completely.

MAKES 10

This spectacular trifle is free of gluten, refined sugar and dairy. Yes, it is indulgent, but Christmas comes around only once a year, and it's truly worth the effort. You will need to start this recipe a day ahead.

TRIFLE WITH COCONUT CREAM AND BERRY JELLY

fresh fruit, such as lychees, strawberries, peaches, blueberries and raspberries, to serve

edible flowers, to decorate (optional)

WHIPPED COCONUT CREAM

2 × 400 ml cans coconut cream

2 tablespoons honey, or to taste

BERRY JELLY

500 g (2½ cups) hulled strawberries

80 g (½ cup) blueberries

175 g (½ cup) honey

juice of 1 lemon

1 tablespoon powdered gelatine

PASTRY CREAM

6 egg yolks

4 tablespoons honey

500 ml (2 cups) coconut milk, plus 3 tablespoons extra

finely grated zest of 2 oranges

1 vanilla pod, split and seeds scraped

3 teaspoons powdered gelatine

Ingredient list continued over page

WHIPPED COCONUT CREAM

Place the unopened cans of coconut cream in a stainless steel mixing bowl and refrigerate overnight.

Open the cans of chilled coconut cream and scoop out the contents into another bowl. Separate the hardened cream layer from the water layer. Place the cream layer and the honey into the chilled bowl. Store the coconut water in a sealed container in the fridge for another use.

Use an electric mixer to whip the hardened coconut cream and honey on high until soft peaks form (3–5 minutes). Allow to set for 40 minutes in the fridge.

BERRY JELLY

Place the strawberries, blueberries, honey and lemon juice in a saucepan with 500 ml (2 cups) of water and bring to the boil over medium heat. Reduce the heat to low and simmer, stirring occasionally, for 15 minutes. Strain.

Pour 3 tablespoons of water into a small cup, sprinkle in the gelatine and soak for 2 minutes. Stir the gelatine through the strawberry mixture until dissolved. Pour the mixture into a deep dish and allow to chill for 4 hours, or until set.

PASTRY CREAM

Whisk the egg yolks and honey until pale and creamy. Whisk in the coconut milk a little at a time until smooth. Transfer to a saucepan, add the orange zest and vanilla pod and seeds and bring to the boil, stirring constantly, until the cream is thick and smooth.

Soak the gelatine with the extra coconut milk for 2 minutes, then mix into the hot pastry cream. Remove from the heat and pour into a bowl. Cover the surface with plastic wrap to prevent a skin from forming. Refrigerate for 1 hour or until completely cold before using.

Recipe continued over page

ALMOND SPONGE

4 eggwhites (about 120 g)

100 g (¼ cup) honey

4 eggs

130 g (1⅓ cups) almond meal

2 tablespoons coconut flour

1 teaspoon baking powder

60 g (½ cup) arrowroot*

3 tablespoons coconut oil, melted

2 tablespoons maple syrup

VANILLA SYRUP

80 g honey

1 vanilla pod, split and seeds scraped

* See Glossary

ALMOND SPONGE

Preheat the oven to 160°C. Grease a 20 cm round cake tin and line the base and sides with baking paper.

Whisk the eggwhites and honey together in a large bowl until soft peaks form. Add the eggs and whisk for 2 minutes until light and fluffy.

Sift the almond meal, coconut flour, baking powder and arrowroot into a separate bowl.

Gently fold the dry ingredients into the eggwhite mixture until well combined. Then fold in the coconut oil and maple syrup. Pour into the prepared tin, smooth the surface with a spatula and sprinkle on the flaked almonds. Bake in the oven for 20–25 minutes until cooked through and lightly golden. Cool in the tin before turning out onto a wire rack.

VANILLA SYRUP

Place 300 ml of water with the honey, vanilla pod and seeds in a small saucepan and bring to the boil. Set aside. Remove the vanilla pod before using.

TO ASSEMBLE

Remove the vanilla pod from the pastry cream, then spoon the pastry cream into a 20 cm round trifle bowl. Cover with a layer of fruit or berries, reserving some to decorate the top. Place the almond sponge cake on top, pressing down lightly. Evenly pour over the vanilla syrup, then spoon on a layer of strawberry jelly. Finish with the whipped coconut cream, the reserved fruit and the edible flowers, if using. Serve chilled.

SERVES 8

> **TIP**
>
> When choosing a coconut cream for the whipped coconut cream, favour organic brands as they contain fewer additives.

Never has there been such an easy Christmas recipe that fits in with the age-old tradition. These are fabulous raw paleo Xmas puddings that you can get the kids to make. For a giggle, Nic and the kids roll these really small and then coat them in carob and call them reindeer poo. You should have seen the look on Nan's face when the girls gave her some reindeer poo . . . Priceless!

RAW CHRISTMAS PUDDINGS

60 g dried figs

2 tablespoons finely grated orange zest

50 g (½ cup) flaxseed meal*

2 tablespoons dried sour cherries

1 teaspoon finely grated ginger

100 g dried apricots

250 g medjool dates, pitted

170 g (1⅔ cups) almond meal

1 teaspoon vanilla extract

¼ teaspoon ground allspice

1 teaspoon ground cinnamon

¼ teaspoon freshly grated nutmeg

3 tablespoons orange juice

1 tablespoon coconut oil

raspberries, to decorate

WHITE ICING

100 g cocoa butter, chopped

100 ml coconut cream

2 tablespoons maple syrup

* See Glossary

Line eight 50 ml capacity dariole moulds or small cups with plastic wrap.

Combine the figs, orange zest, flaxseed meal, cherries, ginger, apricots, dates, almond meal, vanilla and spices in a food processor and process to a crumb-like consistency. Transfer to a large bowl and add the orange juice and coconut oil. Knead until the mixture comes together to form a large ball.

Divide the pudding mixture into eight portions and firmly pack into the prepared moulds. Cover with plastic wrap and place in the fridge for 15 minutes, or until firm. Remove the puddings from the moulds, peel off the plastic wrap and place on a tray.

To make the icing, place the cocoa butter in a heatproof bowl over a saucepan of simmering water and stir until completely melted. Remove from the heat and mix in the coconut cream and maple syrup. Set aside to cool and thicken, stirring occasionally.

Spoon the icing over the puddings and refrigerate for 10–15 minutes until the icing is firm.

Decorate the puddings with the raspberries and serve.

MAKES 8

I know it isn't really a part of Australian culture to serve eggnog at Christmas, but this paleo version provides a great protein hit and is so delicious served chilled that I had to include it. I have suggested coconut milk but you can use any type of nut milk (see page 258). You could even freeze the eggnog in popsicle moulds if you wanted to create an icy Christmas treat.

EGGNOG

4 egg yolks

2 tablespoons coconut sugar* or maple syrup, or to taste

2 × 400 ml cans coconut milk

¼ teaspoon ground cinnamon, plus extra to serve

1 teaspoon freshly grated nutmeg, plus extra to serve

1½–3 tablespoons rum or brandy (optional)

almond milk (to make your own, see page 258), to serve

* See Glossary

Using a hand-held mixer, or an electric mixer with a whisk attachment, whisk the egg yolks for a couple of minutes until doubled in size. Gradually add the coconut sugar or maple syrup and whisk for 1 minute. Set aside.

Combine the coconut milk, cinnamon and nutmeg in a saucepan over medium heat and bring to a gentle simmer. Remove from the heat.

Turn the electric mixer to low and gradually whisk the hot spiced coconut milk into the egg yolk mixture until well combined.

Pour the mixture into a clean saucepan and stir gently but constantly over low heat for 5–10 minutes, or until the mixture thickens and coats the back of the spoon. Be patient with this process; if you turn the heat up too high or don't stir, the mixture might turn into scrambled eggs. Remove from the heat and mix in some rum or brandy, if using. Set the pan over a bowl of iced water to stop the cooking process, stirring occasionally for 2 minutes. (Be careful, you don't want water overflowing into the eggnog!). Cover with plastic wrap and place in the fridge to chill. (The longer you let it chill, the thicker it will become.)

Before serving, add the desired amount of almond milk to thin the eggnog and sprinkle with some extra nutmeg and cinnamon.

SERVES 4

GLOSSARY

ADOBO SAUCE

Adobo is a type of sauce or marinade widely used in Latin American cuisine. Its main ingredients usually include tomatoes, onions, chillies, garlic, vinegar and spices. Adobo sauce can be bought at gourmet food stores and some supermarkets.

ALMOND BUTTER

A spread made from raw or toasted almonds, almond butter is a great alternative to peanut butter as it contains more fibre, calcium, potassium and iron, with half of the saturated fat. It's available at health food stores and many supermarkets.

APPLE CIDER VINEGAR

I use raw, organic apple cider vinegar, which is sometimes labelled 'apple cider vinegar with mother'. The 'mother' is made of enzymes and bacteria and has a cobweb-like appearance. Apple cider vinegar is rich in potassium and is believed to help clear up skin conditions. I love using it in dressings and stocks and often dilute some in warm water to make a great morning drink. Raw apple cider vinegar can be found at health food stores.

ARROWROOT

Arrowroot is a starch made from the roots of several tropical plants, including tapioca and cassava. It is gluten free and is great for making paleo-friendly pizza bases, tortillas, cakes and pastry. It can be found at health food stores and some supermarkets.

BONITO FLAKES

Bonito flakes are made from the bonito fish, which is like a small tuna. The fish is smoked, fermented, dried and shaved, and the end product looks similar to wood shavings. Bonito flakes are used to garnish Japanese dishes, to make sauces such as ponzu, soups such as miso and to make the Japanese stock, dashi. You can find bonito flakes in Asian food stores.

BUCKWHEAT

Buckwheat is the seed of a flowering fruit that is related to rhubarb and sorrel. It is gluten free and is a popular substitute for wheat. Buckwheat is high in protein, containing all nine essential amino acids, including lysine. It is also rich in iron, antioxidants, magnesium, zinc, copper and niacin. Try adding buckwheat to salads or using it instead of rice or porridge. You can also buy buckwheat in flour form, which is great for gluten-free baking. Look for buckwheat in health food stores and some supermarkets.

CACAO AND CAROB POWDERS

Cacao powder comes from cacao beans that are fermented, dried, peeled and then cold pressed to extract about 75 per cent of the cacao butter, leaving a dark brown paste. After drying, the remaining cacao solids are processed to make fine, unsweetened cacao powder. Cacao powder is rich in antioxidants and also contains zinc, calcium, iron, copper, sulphur, potassium and caffeine. Carob powder is made from the pod of the carob tree and is a great substitute for cacao if you want to avoid caffeine. You can add cacao or carob powder to your smoothies, tea, coffee, protein drinks, desserts or anything else you can think of. I choose raw, organic cacao and carob powders and these can be found at health food stores.

CHIA SEEDS

Chia seeds come from a Latin American plant and they pack a huge punch when it comes to nutrients. They are a great source of protein and also contain omega-3 and omega-6 fatty acids, calcium, potassium, iron and magnesium. When placed in liquid, chia seeds swell to 17 times their original size, so they are a great substitute for traditional thickening agents like cornflour. I love sprinkling chia seeds into smoothies, muesli, salads and desserts. You can buy them from health food stores and supermarkets.

CHIPOTLE CHILLIES

Chipotle chillies are smoke-dried jalapeños and are commonly used in Mexican cooking. They are often sold in jars or tins immersed in adobo sauce (see page 284). They impart a mild but earthy spiciness to dishes and are absolutely delicious when pureed and mixed through homemade aioli (page 172). You can also buy chipotle chillies in dried, powdered form. Look for them at Central and South American food stores, as well as some gourmet food stores.

COCONUTS

Young coconuts are harvested at around 5–7 months and are usually white in colour. The best way to open one is to cut a circle in the top using a large knife and then prise this circle off. The amount of coconut water inside varies, but is usually around 250 ml. It is a good source of potassium and makes a refreshing drink on a hot day. Once you've poured the water out of the coconut, you can scoop out the soft flesh using a spoon. Look for young coconuts at Asian food stores and health food stores.

Coconut aminos is made from the raw sap of the coconut tree, which is naturally aged and blended with sea salt. It is a great alternative to soy sauce as it has a higher amino acid content and no gluten. It is also slightly less salty than tamari. You'll find coconut aminos in health food stores.

Coconut flour is made from dried coconut meal and is a natural by-product of coconut milk production. It is gluten-free and rich in protein, fibre and fat. Coconut flour is much more absorbent than wheat flour – you only need about one-third the amount and will need to use more eggs and liquid, such as coconut milk. It's best to start off by using recipes that are built around coconut flour rather than trying to experiment on your own. It is available from health food stores.

Coconut sugar is produced from the sap of cut flower buds on the coconut palm and is subtly sweet with a caramel flavour. It is a good alternative to refined cane sugar as it has a lower GI and a high mineral content. Like all sweeteners, I use coconut sugar sparingly. You will find it at health food stores.

Coconut water is the white liquid found inside young coconuts. It is high in amino acids, enzymes, dietary fibre, vitamin C and minerals such as potassium, magnesium and manganese, while also being low in cholesterol and chlorides. Coconut water is great for smoothies, drinks, ice cream or even drinking on its own on a summer's day. You will find coconut water at health food stores and some supermarkets – make sure you check the label carefully as some brands contain added sugar and preservatives.

DRIED SHRIMP

Available from Asian food stores and some supermarkets, dried shrimp are used in many different Asian cuisines. They shrink dramatically during the process of sun drying and only need to be used sparingly as they impart quite a strong umami flavour.

DUCK FAT

See Fats

DULSE FLAKES

Dulse flakes are made from a red algae that grows on the northern coasts of the Atlantic and Pacific oceans. It is rich in protein and a good source of many vitamins and minerals, including iodine. I like sprinkling some dulse flakes into nori rolls and they are also great in dressings or added to salads and soups. Look for dulse flakes at health food stores, Asian food stores or online.

EGGS

The best eggs come from free-range chickens, which are allowed to roam freely outside in the sunshine, eat insects and plants, and have a far healthier and happier life than those trapped in cages. Free-range eggs taste better, have stronger shells, are less runny, and have firmer and brighter yolks. They also contain less cholesterol and saturated fat than caged eggs, and have higher levels of vitamin A, E and D, protein, beta-carotene and omega-3 fatty acids. I use extra-large eggs in my recipes.

FATS

I use either coconut oil or good-quality animal fats for cooking as they have high smoke points (meaning they do not oxidise at high temperatures). Some of my favourite animal fats to use are ghee (clarified butter), lard (pork fat), tallow (rendered beef fat), rendered chicken fat and duck fat. Ghee is available from Indian food stores and some supermarkets. It has had the milk solids removed so is very low in lactose. Always look for ghee from grass-fed cows. Lard, tallow, rendered chicken fat and duck fat may be harder to find – ask at your local butcher or meat supplier, or you can also look online for meat suppliers who sell them. Extra-virgin olive oil is fantastic for salad dressings or for drizzling over finished dishes

FLAXSEEDS

Also known as linseeds, flaxseeds are one of the most concentrated plant sources of omega-3 fats. They can be ground up into flaxseed meal and also used to create oil. Care needs to be taken in the storage of flaxseed products as they contain unsaturated fat and can go rancid if they aren't stored in an airtight container in a cool place. It is hard to absorb the nutrients in whole flaxseeds as they have a hard outer shell, so for maximum nutrition, it is best to consume them in ground or oil form. Flaxseed meal or oil can be added to muffins, muesli or smoothies for a fibre, antioxidant and omega-3 boost. Flaxseed products can be found at health food stores, as well as some supermarkets and pharmacies.

GELATINE

I always choose gelatine sourced from organic, grass-fed beef. Vegetarian substitutes for gelatine include agar agar and carrageen, which are made from two different types of seaweed. Sometimes these aren't as strong as regular gelatine, so you may need to increase the quantity. Some kosher gelatines are also vegan. You can buy gelatine made from organic, grass-fed beef, agar agar and carrageen from health food stores or online.

GHEE
See Fats

GOJI BERRIES

Goji berries are mainly grown in China, Mongolia and Tibet. They are bright pink and have a mild, tangy taste that is slightly sweet and sour. Goji berries are usually sold in dried form and have the same kind of shape and chewy texture as raisins. They contain all the essential amino acids and have the highest concentration of protein of any fruit. They also contain vitamin C, carotenoids, fibre, iron, calcium, zinc, selenium and many other important trace minerals. Goji berries are great for adding to muesli, desserts, sweet sauces and puddings. Goji berry powder is also available and can be stirred directly into juices, herbal teas, coconut water or plain water. Goji berries can be found at your local supermarket or health food store.

HABANERO CHILLIES

Habaneros are super hot chillies that are widely used in Mexican cuisine. They are small and stubby with thin, waxy flesh and a fruity flavour. You'll find them in Central and South American food stores, as well as some gourmet food stores.

HONEY AND MAPLE SYRUP

I rarely use sweeteners in my cooking, but when I do I usually opt for honey or maple syrup. I always choose raw, organic honey as it tastes better, is unprocessed and is produced in rural areas where there is much less pollution. Make sure that you choose a 100 per cent pure maple syrup (made from boiling down the sap of maple trees) rather than imitation maple-flavoured sugar syrup.

JAMAICA (DRIED HIBISCUS)

Jamaica is used in many parts of the world to make hibiscus tea – an infusion of a particular part of the hibiscus flower that has been collected and dried. The tea has a tart cranberry flavour and is believed to help people with high blood pressure. Jamaica can be found at health food stores.

KAFFIR LIME LEAVES

Kaffir lime leaves have a mysterious smell unlike any other citrus. The leaves give a wholesome, lemony essence to your dishes and are fabulous for flavouring curry pastes. Fresh kaffir lime leaves can be found at Asian food stores.

KELP NOODLES

Kelp noodles are clear noodles made from seaweed. They contain more than 70 nutrients and minerals, including iodine, potassium, magnesium, calcium, iron and more than 21 amino acids. Kelp noodles are great for stir-fries, casseroles, soups and salads. You can find them at heath food stores.

KOHLRABI

A member of the brassica family, the taste and texture of kohlrabi is similar to that of broccoli stem. It can be eaten both raw and cooked and is popular in Germany and parts of India. You can find kohlrabi at greengrocers and some supermarkets.

LARD

See Fats

LICORICE ROOT POWDER

When ground into a powder, licorice root has a slightly sweet flavour and can be added to smoothies, drinks and desserts. Licorice root has been used in Chinese medicine for many years and is believed to help with a wide range of conditions, including digestive problems. Licorice root powder can be found at health food stores.

LIQUID SMOKE

Liquid smoke is produced by passing smoke through a tube from a combustion chamber filled with wood chips to a condenser. It can be added as a seasoning to dishes to impart a smoky flavour. Liquid smoke is available from gourmet food and barbecue stores.

LSA

LSA stands for linseed, sunflower seed and almond meal and it can be added to smoothies, sprinkled on salads and fruit and added to just about any meal for a protein and vitamin boost. It is high in fibre, essential fatty acids, B vitamins, magnesium and calcium. LSA should be stored in the fridge as it is high in unsaturated fats, which can go rancid. You can buy LSA from health food stores or supermarkets.

MACA POWDER

Maca is a rainforest herb that is high in protein and other nutrients. It is believed to increase energy and support the immune system. Try adding a spoonful of maca powder to your smoothies for a protein boost.

MÂCHE

Also known as corn lettuce or lamb's lettuce, mâche is a European salad green with a sweet flavour. It is best enjoyed raw in a salad and is available from greengrocers.

MEAT

I always source the absolute best quality meat I can find – organic, pasture-raised beef and pork, and organic, free-range chicken. It really is worth paying a little extra for, as you know that the quality of the protein is second to none, that the animals have led happy lives and haven't been injected full of hormones and antibiotics and that the flavour will always be amazing. If you don't have a good butcher near you, there are lots of online stores that will deliver to your door.

MUSTARD

My preferred mustard is my own homemade fermented mustard (page 177) but if you don't have time to make your own, you can substitute a good-quality wholegrain or Dijon mustard. Just make sure you check the label as some mustards have added sugar and gluten.

NORI SHEETS

Nori is a dark green, paper-like, toasted seaweed used for most kinds of sushi and other Japanese dishes. Nori provides an abundance of essential nutrients and is rich in vitamins, iron, minerals, amino acids, omega-3 and omega-6, and antioxidants. Nori sheets are commonly used to roll sushi, but they can also be shredded and added to salads, soups, and fish, meat and vegetable dishes. You can buy nori sheets from Asian food stores and most supermarkets.

POMEGRANATE MOLASSES

Pomegranate molasses is a beautifully thick, tangy and glossy reduction of pomegranate juice that has a sweet and sour flavour and is rich in antioxidants. Pomegranate molasses is used in Middle Eastern countries for glazing meat and chicken before roasting, and in sauces, salad dressings and marinades. Pomegranate molasses is available from Middle Eastern grocers and some delis.

PROBIOTIC CAPSULES

Probiotic capsules contain live bacteria that can help to regulate digestion, clear up yeast infections and assist with conditions such as irritable bowel syndrome. These capsules need to be kept in the fridge. They can be swallowed whole, or opened up and used to ferment drinks such as kefir (page 256). Probiotic capsules can be found at pharmacies and health food stores.

QUINOA

Quinoa is a South American crop and is actually a seed rather than a grain. It is gluten free and contains high levels of protein, as well as some calcium, phosphorus and iron. Quinoa is available in many different varieties, including white, red and black, and each one has a subtly different flavour. It is also available as flakes and flour. You can find it at supermarkets and health food stores.

SALT

I like to use sea salt or Himalayan salt in my cooking, as they are less processed than table salt, contain more minerals and have a lovely crunchy texture. Himalayan salt is light pink in colour due to the presence of a number of different minerals, including iron, magnesium, calcium and copper. You can purchase both sea salt and Himalayan salt at supermarkets and health food stores.

SCOTCH BONNETS

Scotch bonnets are a type of chilli that are very hot and commonly used in west African, Jamaican and Haitian cuisines, among many others. Similar in appearance to habanero chillies, they have a slightly sweeter flavour. Scotch bonnets are available from gourmet food stores.

SHRIMP PASTE

Shrimp paste is used in many different Asian cuisines and is an essential ingredient in numerous curries and sauces. It is made from tiny shrimp that are salted, fermented, then ground into a smooth paste and sun dried. Shrimp paste has a very powerful smell and taste, so should only be used in small quantities. You can find it in Asian food stores and some supermarkets.

SPIRULINA

Spirulina is a microscopic blue-green algae. It's high in protein and contains many vitamins and minerals, including vitamins A and B, and iron. Spirulina is believed to be good for your teeth, hair, skin and immune system. It is usually sold in powdered form and is great to use in smoothies, shakes, muesli, juices, drinks and desserts. You can buy spirulina from heath food stores and some supermarkets.

TAHINI

Tahini is a paste made from ground sesame seeds and has a smooth, creamy texture. It is an excellent source of protein, copper and manganese and a good source of calcium, magnesium, iron, phosphorus, vitamin B1, zinc, selenium and essential fatty acids. Tahini is a well-known ingredient in North African, Greek, Turkish, and Middle Eastern cuisine. It is used to make hummus, dips and salad dressings. I prefer unhulled tahini, which has a stronger flavour, but there are also hulled varieties available, as well as black tahini made from black sesame seeds. You can find tahini in supermarkets and heath food stores.

TALLOW
See Fats

TAMARI

Tamari is made with whole, fermented soybeans. It is similar to soy sauce, but is richer and less salty and contains no wheat, so is gluten free. Tamari is mostly used in Asian cuisines and is perfect for stir-fries, marinades, dressings, soups and dipping sauces. You can find it in supermarkets and Asian food stores.

TAMARIND

Tamarind paste is made from the pods of the tamarind tree and is used as a souring agent, particularly in Indian dishes, chutneys and curries. It is also used to flavour pulse or rice dishes, or as an ingredient in sauces and side dishes for pork, chicken and fish. Tamarind has a mild laxative effect. It can be found at Asian food stores and some supermarkets.

TAPIOCA FLOUR

Tapioca flour is made by grinding up the dried root of the manioc (also known as cassava) plant. It is similar to arrowroot and can be used to thicken dishes or in gluten-free baking. You can find tapioca flour at health food stores and some supermarkets.

TOMATILLOS

Widely used in Mexican cuisine, the tomatillo is a member of the deadly nightshade family and has a bright green colour and tart flavour. They are used to make sauces, jams and preserves. Tomatillos can be found fresh or preserved in specialty food stores.

VEGETABLE STARTER CULTURE

A vegetable starter culture is a preparation used to kick-start the fermentation process when culturing vegetables (see pages 171, 174 and 178). I prefer to use a broad-spectrum starter sourced from organic vegetables rather than one grown from dairy sources, as this ensures your fermented product will contain the highest number of living, active bacteria and will produce consistently successful results free of pathogens. Vegetable starter culture usually comes in sachets and can be purchased at health food stores or online.

YACON SYRUP

Extracted from the roots of the South American yacon plant, this syrup is a sweetener that is low in sugar and calories. It has a dark colour and a caramel flavour and can be found at health food stores.

YOUNG COCONUTS

See Coconuts

THANK YOU

Once again thank you to my beautiful partner in life and love, Nicola. I am seriously the luckiest bloke on the planet.

To my bunnies, Indii and Chilli – you know this book wouldn't have come about if it weren't for you. I love you both so much and you are both so unique in your own special ways.

To Anson Smart (photography) and David Morgan (styling) – once again you fellas have nailed it. It was a long time between drinks for us, but I am glad you opened up a spot in your busy schedule to make this book absolutely gorgeous.

To Mark Roper (photography) and Deb Kaloper (styling) – thanks for the extra food shots. You are both magicians.

To Steve Brown (photography) and Trish Heagerty (styling) – thanks for creating a wonderful cover and some great lifestyle images. I think we set the record for the quickest cover shoot in history!

To Mary Small, the coolest book publisher in the Southern Hemisphere – keep on standing out from the pack and delivering books that will help change the world.

To Jane Winning – thanks once again for making sure all my recipes are tested for everyone cooking from the book.

To Megan Johnston – thank you for your careful and thorough editing.

To Kirby Armstrong – thanks again for creating a fabulous design for the book.

To Monica and Jacinta Cannataci – girls, I can't thank you enough for again giving up your time to help me out on my passion projects. It is great watching you evolve.

To Phil Davenport – mate, thanks for jumping on the tools when needed. It's not every day you get a world class chef to help out.

To Charlotte Ree – if you thought you were busy with *Healthy Every Day*, well we have just upped the ante … go get 'em!

To Mum – thanks for passing on your love of cooking.

And finally to my mentors and the trailblazers in health and nutrition, I couldn't have done it without you: Nora Gedgaudas, Pete Melov, Rudy Eckhardt, Pete Bablis, William (Bill) Davis, David Perlmutter, Gary Taubes, Frank Lipman, David Gillespie, Ben Balzer, Loren Cordain, Bruce Fife, Mat Lalonde, Martha Herbert, Joseph Mercola, Sally Fallon, Dr Natasha Campbell-McBride, Kitsa Yanniotis and Donna Gates.

INDEX